I want you to click now.

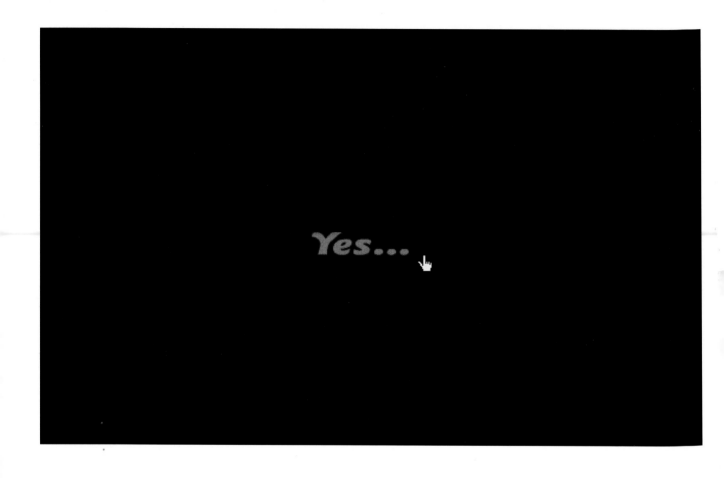

NOW LOADING . . .

GINGKO PRESS

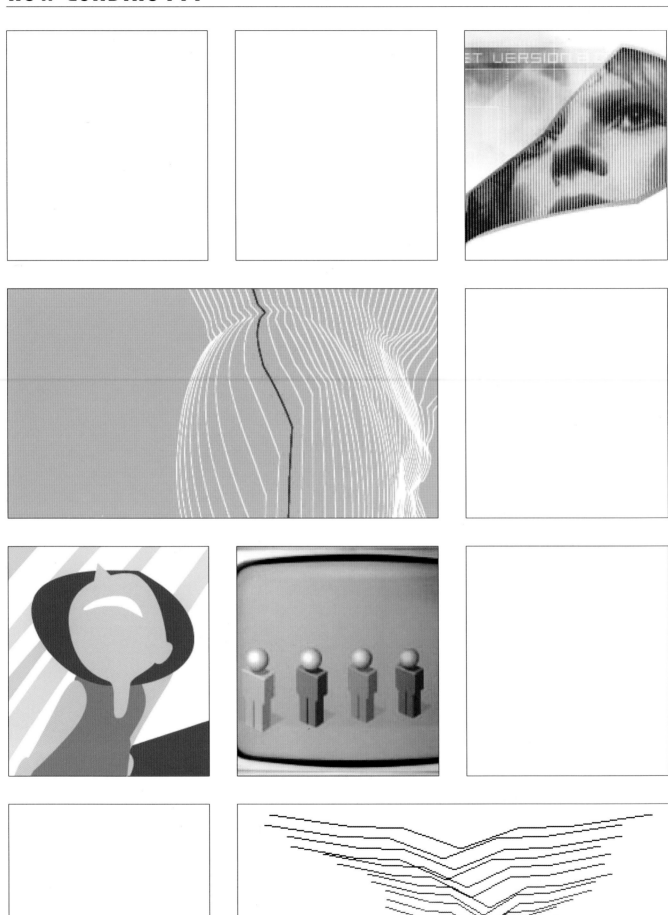

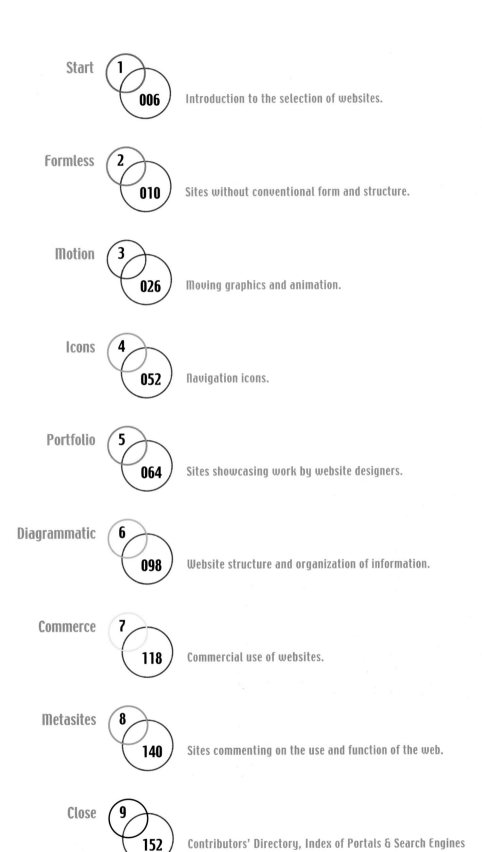

this immediate and visual mode of communication seems to rule out a common assumption that all web broadcasting will eventually turn into live video feed.) Exploring the nature of this graphic language is one of the objectives of this volume. Which visual communication tools are unique to web design? How and where do design and content meet? Working within the parameters of the web, what new design has resulted? For example, of paramount importance in website construction and organization are simplicity of use and speed of navigation. A central graphic may double as the site's central navigational tool. All the links are quite close and localized into a relatively small area of the homepage, enabling the user to understand the scope and content of the entire site quickly and without having to fumble through several pages (c.f., www.bowienet.com, pages 120–121).

The effectiveness and use of standard graphic elements are put to the test in this new context. Photography on the web presents one such challenge: it is very susceptible to being overpowered by the vivid solid colors available on the computer screen. The existing strategies for using photography in web design can only be relied on to a certain extent before a different approach to design becomes necessary. Layout, dimension, and sequencing as they are effected in print media also require some re-working when applied to "pages" of a website. Unlike print media, in which photography can be used to help move the viewer's eyes up, down, across and onto the next page, websites utilize mobile

The web has created an audience of users who are astute to visual design, critical of graphics, sensitive to visual language, and insatiable. Graphic design, on the whole, probably hasn't ever enjoyed such an extensive popular appreciation. Granted, the design element of websites is assessed by lay users wholly on the merit of its initial allure and newness. There is a ready supply of tiling graphics, animated texts, and sophisticated menu bars, all provided in an effort to trump the sophistication of other sites.

In an ever-growing trend, graphic design itself can now play a double role as "content". The movement is toward a greater and popular familiarity with a "graphic language"—wherein a user can fully experience a website with little to no "text" per se. (The tendency toward elements, continually moving parts, and graphics—a new arena that demands a whole different way of looking at the picture field. The selection of color with the computer is far greater than that in print media—though there are technical, and even stylistic limitations to the digital color palette. The key difference in the palette of the two media, however, is not a matter of color separation or resolution. Color on the computer monitor is illuminated: light shines *through* the color. What designers have experienced since the start of routine desktop design work has now expanded to a general audience. The tools of the trade have similarly become available to the public. A website generated by a small team, or even one person, can have the same refinement and visual appeal as a professionally designed site and be just as accessible. Because of its relative newness, web design doesn't have the same level of market segmentation that is clearly visible across the spectrum of advertising, entertainment media, and the visual arts.

Website Selection and "What is there to see?"

On first glance, good design can look deceptively simple and familiar, almost as though it had always existed. Or, better still, it doesn't look *designed* at all. So finding a well-designed website can be quite a tricky task, especially when trying to set aside personal preferences and to remain open to innovative work. Web design, when compared to other media and arts, is still in its infancy. Thus, there is inevitably a lot of excitement and experimentation, but also a great deal of design that can

be considered nothing more than an exploitation of software tools and plug-ins for flashy effects. The main criteria for the selection of sites in this volume are: their effectiveness in problem solving, communication, and function, and their originality—perennial themes of graphic design, in all media.

In the expository texts that accompany the sites featured here, discussion of software has been avoided, except when an understanding of the creator's use of software illuminates the aesthetic nature of the work. In general, the sites selected do not make use of software and technology just for the sake of using software and technology, but as a vehicle to further larger aims. The basic business of this book is not to explicate technical issues or to point out the limitations of web media; rather, the intention here is to demonstrate design ideas by providing a set of examples from a number of innovative creators. Not just new web design, but *good* new web design. This was the fundamental standard for the selection of sites—a standard that narrowed the choices considerably. Fussy sites with a lot of noisy buzzers and attention-grabbing demonstration graphics have been passed over here, not only in the name of good taste. Instead, the focus is on sites that have depth of design and character.

This book, in other words, is about the aesthetics of web design. Within the larger realms of graphic design, and design in general, a discussion of web aesthetics makes sense, as the lessons learned in web design are now beginning to offer applications to other media. Many of the designers creating for the web continue to work with other media, all the while being influenced by web design. Several of the contributors to this volume hold that there is no difference between designing for the web and designing for any other medium. This may be quite true. But as we explore the developments in visual organization, communication through web graphics, and graphics that are particular to the web, we begin to discern the various paths of the web's visual language. The examples presented in this book help to guide us toward that end.

The spare and simple presentation of the sites here is intended to be as non-intrusive, as *invisible* as possible, to allow the individual images to remain uncluttered by book design, and to let the labors of each designer and creator be as apparent as possible to the viewer. Both the layouts and the accompanying texts are geared toward elucidating the goals of these creators.

Killing Realtime

A number of website-design firms have been waiting in the wings for the advent of the much-heralded broadband connections with sophisticated sites that will rival all present concepts of interactivity and engage super levels of heightened virtual reality. In terms of design and function, this advance toward virtual liberty may well serve to exacerbate the problem of vapid and overly artful websites. In this medium, where web creators and users alike are still spellbound by the tools

of the trade, the little that will last in the legacy of website design will most likely be websites that are comparatively reserved in their use of flashy design, and sedate in their approach to virtual-interactive environments. This volume presents the work of several creators who are striving to develop the craft of website design and to see it for what it is, in all its potential incarnations.

Who's Steering this Thing, Anyway?

Perhaps the greatest capability that the web provides is user-to-user interaction: a free and unregulated community of people interacting without mediation or censorship. On-line trading and file swapping are the epitome of laissez-faire. Within this framework, websites are simply channels or nodes, like signposts, where users may gather. But serious issues arise when even the web becomes systematized and regulated by any one force, whether it's a commercial interest, a software monopoly, or the universal acceptance of standards of web design.

An understanding of web aesthetics begins with questions like, "Who has created this visual language?"; "Can't there be other ways of communicating between users?" and "What are the limitations and restrictions of this system?" Are we to see a set of navigation tools and a readily identifiable set of forms with clearly labeled and reliable functions as a rigid methodology for interpretation and understanding? This may be a danger of web aesthetics. Until there is a broad and deep familiarity with the new lexicon of web graphics, navigation, and function, the general user is in a position to be swayed by a limited range of highly coded images, which might be mistaken for "the truth." Looking at web graphics and discussing the aesthetics behind them is one way of questioning, holding their "truth" up for examination. And once there is some articulation of this—once its rules are laid bare—then it all becomes transparent, allowing for transgression, for those rules to be broken. Thus, the final chapter of websites in this volume is "Metasites": sites that comment on the web itself. In these sites, everything that has come to be accepted as standard, recognizable, safe, and the manner in which things are done with regard to website design is summarily called into question.

Even with dazzling animation of graphics, there is an overarching tendency toward organization and recognizable forms and structures that have some representation outside of the virtual world. There are several websites (some of which make up the first chapter in this volume) that allow the user to create graphics. Before the average user begins to have fixed ideas about how a website should look, or what is meant by web graphics, before he or she begins to expect highly polished design and graphic elements as the standard, this first chapter will set up a foil for everything that follows in the volume. At the very least, the aim here is to focus our attention on the artful nature of graphics, and to urge users to maintain a constant state of suspicion.

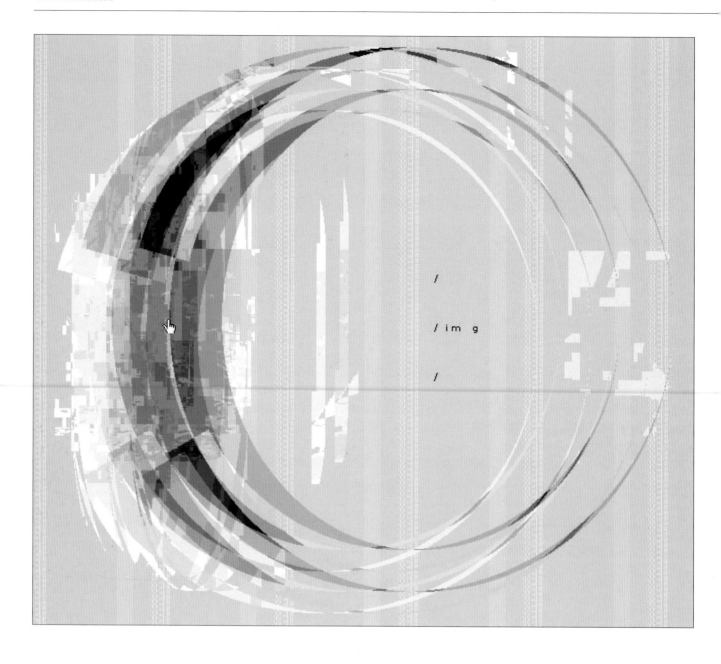

www.meta.am

The shimmering, metallic planes of the first pages in the Meta.Am site resemble a three-dimensional space of undistinguished form. Further in the site reveals that the initial concentric, overlapping half-circles seem to have no dimension, nor are they meant to represent anything. The site's creator, Meta, remarks of the graphics, "I wanted the viewer to have a sense of looking into and exploring a series of elements suspended in space, rather than a series of graphic elements laid out on a page, perhaps anticipating a time when the World Wide Web will indeed be perceived as navigation in three-dimensional space." The site makes available MP3s and graphics for downloading, including a series of single-color computer-generated images. Meta explains that the barely legible navigation text (words with missing letters) serves as a reminder of the constant potential for error and experimentation, so fundamental to the process of design. For Meta, these elements provide a means of "humanizing the machine." This fallible machine is relied upon to provide a stream of randomly paired images and texts in another section of the site—for example, a snapshot of a winding staircase and a newsclip about a cow taken from some regional tabloid. The succession of these pairings (images and texts have been culled from various sources, both suspect and "legitimate") is apparently endless. As can happen easily, the relationship between the photographs and the texts gets strained, bringing us back to the primary graphics of the site, which are formless themselves.

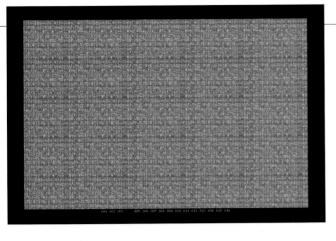

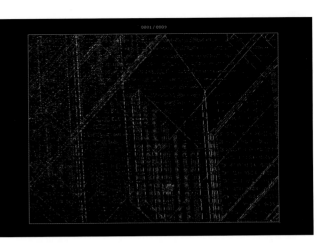

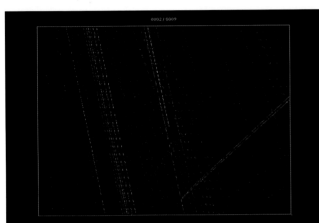

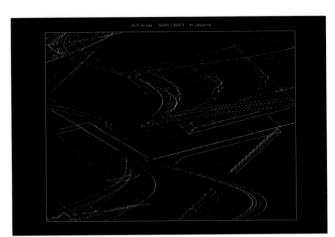

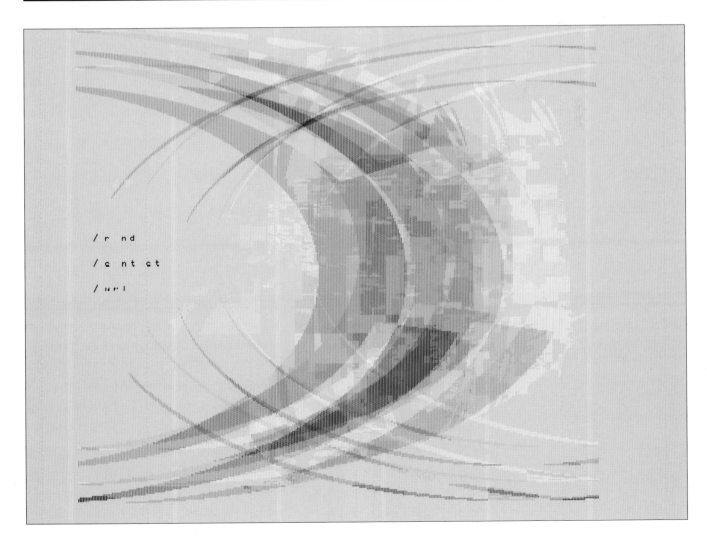

/ r nd

/ c nt ct

/ u r l

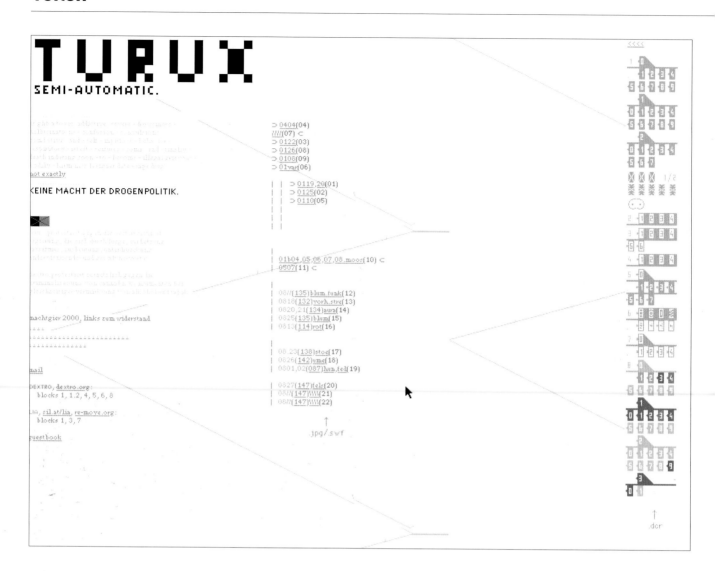

Vienna
www.turux.org

In the Turux website, what you bring to the site is the content that you will uncover. Created by the team of Dextro (www.dextro.org) and Lia (www.re-move.org), the site presents a series of blocks, which generate graphic elements and images corresponding to the presence and movement of the user's mouse. Each block has a different way of responding to the user's stimulus. The graphics are generated in a stream, pressing the user for further movement and interaction. In this regard, the user becomes engaged in unpredictable and unprogrammed action, and the picture that is produced in the process becomes a tangential record. Dextro outlines the directives of the site: "To provide tools for creating pictures. Escape our own predictability. Show an open field rather than define our territory. . . ." The mode of production in the Turux site manages to escape systems, programs, and categorizations, challenging the user to see things newly.

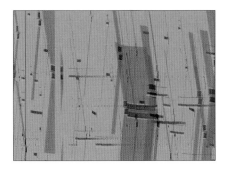
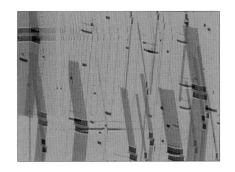
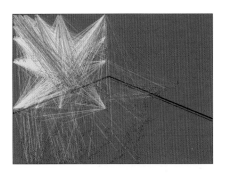
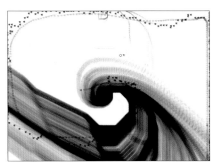
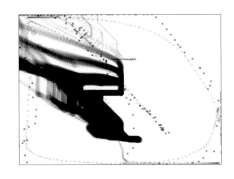
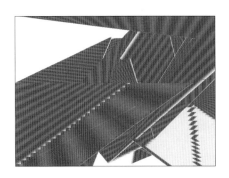
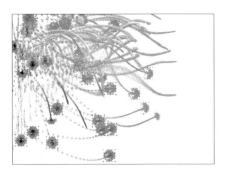

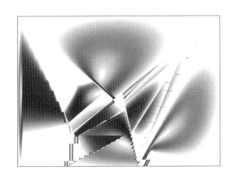
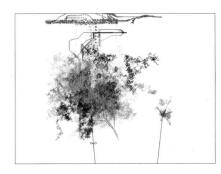
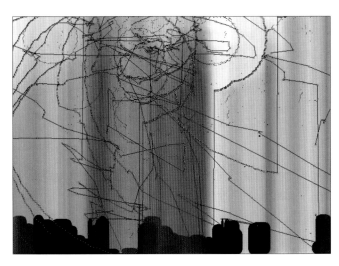
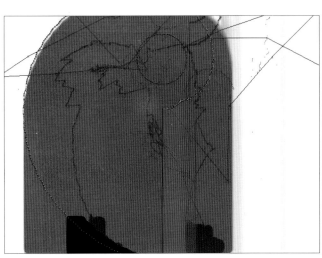

DEXTRO

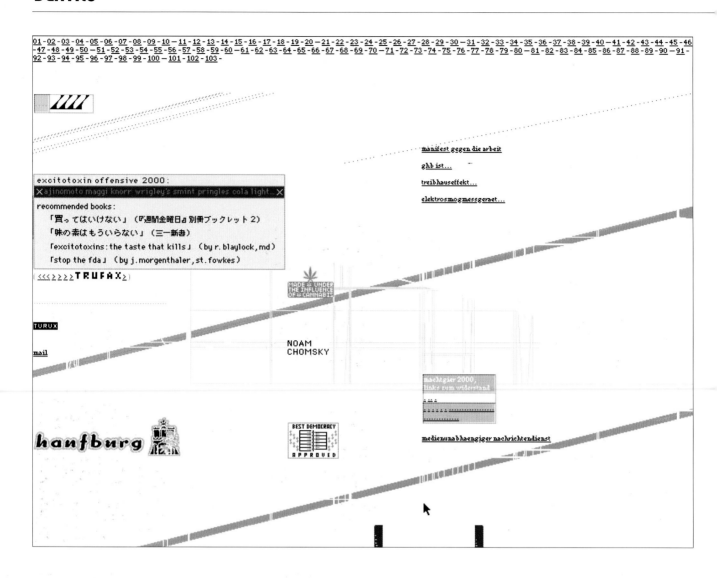

Vienna
www.dextro.org

Dextro.org, a site independent from the collaboration with Lia on Turux.org, presents a similar immediacy of engagement. Here, though, the functions, numbered in succession across the top of the main interface, provide more maneuvers for manipulating and creating images. The complete reliance on digital imagery here allows for greater freedom with exploring the formless. The user's cursor draws lines like graffiti etched in paint. As the eponymous name of the site implies, the focus of this site is turned inward, toward its creator, extending the process of the Turux.org site into more of a personal exploration. Prominently displayed in the center of the main navigation is the adviso: "Created under the influence of cannibis," which Dextro describes as "the gateway to creativity." The site is given great import by Dextro, who sees Dextro.org and Turux.org as his exploration of the meaning of life. Whether the website is successful in moving its creator toward his goal is irrelevant. It remains a process and movement of unlimited possible directions.

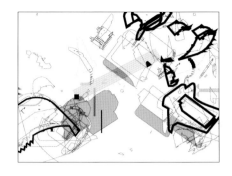

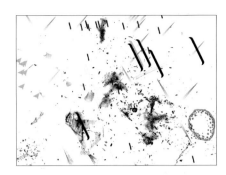

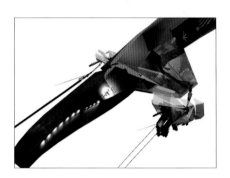

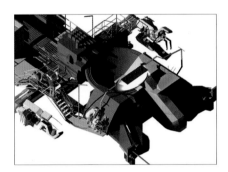
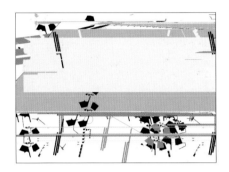
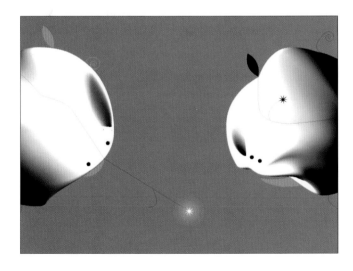
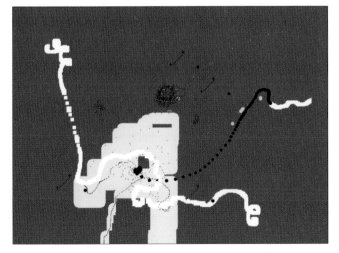
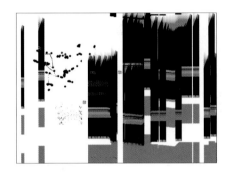
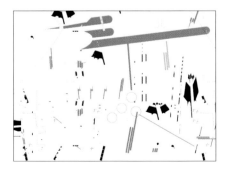
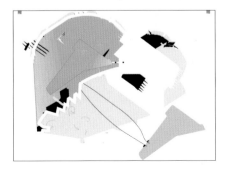
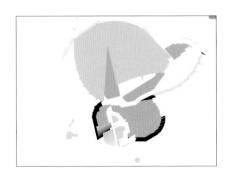

Vienna
www.re-move.org

"The main purpose is to make the beauty of mathematics visible somehow," writes site-creator Lia of Re:move. There are eight functions on the site that allow the user to create images interactively. The toolbar that runs below the interface for each function is a set of buttons, most of them unnamed, that allow the user to adjust the parameters of movement, frequency, range, angle, and the number of "players" or graphic elements; without the benefit of designations, the user has to deduce what the buttons correspond to. In reference to the almost complete lack of instructional or expository text in the site's interface, Lia writes, "People should be able to see the work and get their own ideas about it. They should have the possibility to experience (and to influence interactively) each part, employing their own attitudes, which is why the users are not given exact guidelines for what to do or not to do in using the site." This allows for a wide-open exchange of ideas about the processes and laws that govern both nature and mathematics. Nature is ordered by a symmetry that is disturbed by randomness, but even these disturbances have their inherent patterns. Experiments with Re:move are, in a sense, reflections of this, with the user himself serving as the element of disruption. What may at first appear to be random behavior might well (as the user may discover) turn out to be patterned behavior. The user's movement of the cursor is interpreted by the coding in the site to make, move, and prompt change in the lines, patterns, and shapes on the screen. In just a few moments, an image is created. That image continually evolves, regardless of whether it is "complete," regardless of whether the user continues to manipulate the mouse, and regardless of what the user anticipates.

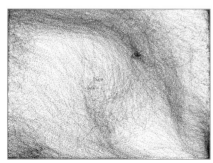
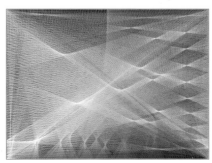
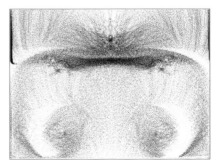

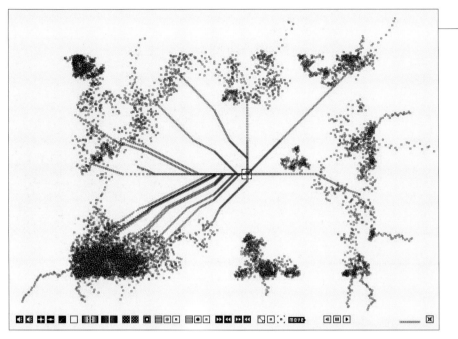

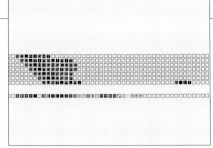

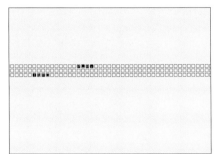

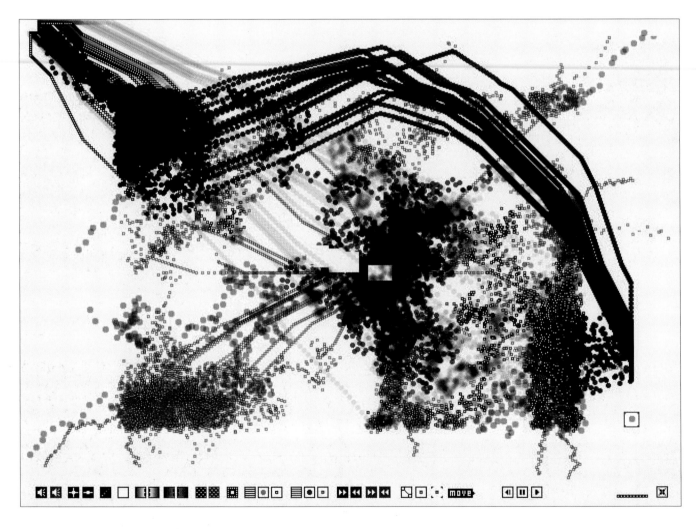

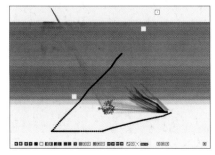

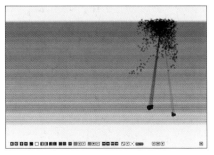

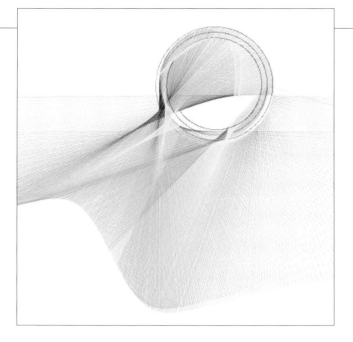
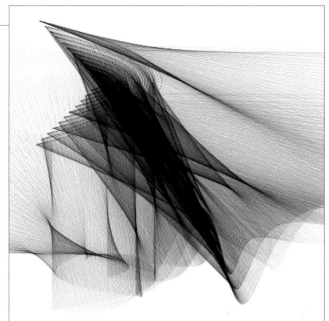
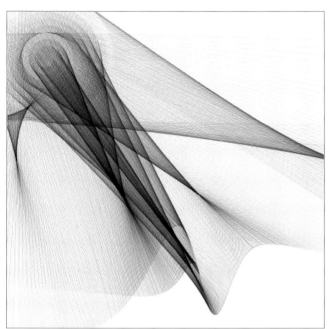
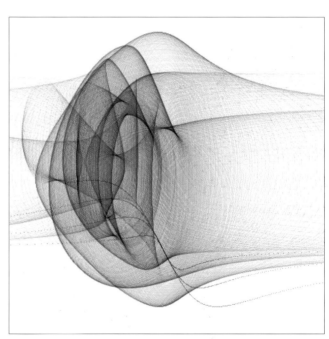
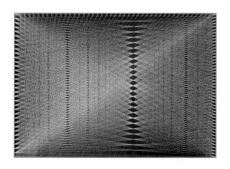

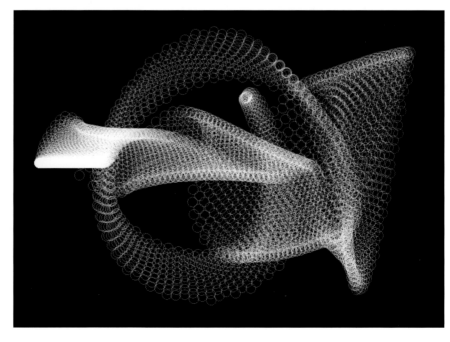

uncontrol

is an interactive exercise that explores
the themes of anthropomorphism and kinetics.

using Macromedia **Flash**, I developed experiments
that express these themes using only basic forms:
lines, splines, rectangles, and circles.

✉ manatee@uncontrol.com

experiments   ? 0 1 2 3 4 5 6 7 8 9 10 11 12 13 14 draw

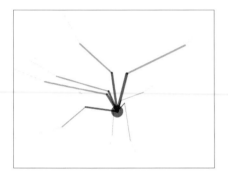

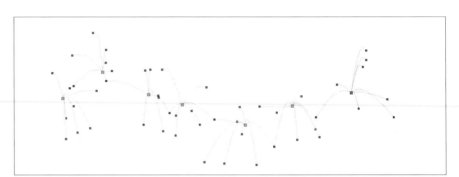

www.uncontrol.com

Despite the sedate and understated design of Uncontrol, the row of numbers across the screen link to a series of experiments using Macromedia Flash and Director. Born of creator Manual Tan's interest in the mechanics and structure of things, this site serves as an exploration of the laws of nature and kinetics. Each experiment reveals some structure or graphic elements in a causal relationship, which is animated by Uncontrol. The site developed from earlier experiments with creating algorithimic programs in Macromedia Director. The elements that Tan generated were beyond control; hence the name of the site. This is Tan's attempt to understand the kinetics found in everyday life—in such basic acts as walking. The user can establish various parameters, such as restricting movement or changing the movement's direction, which is, in effect, a way for the user to study movement and the relationship of objects using the models that are provided. The pared-down look of the site itself keeps the mood contemplative and underscores its tutorial nature. The moving images that result are further examples of unspecified and formless imagery that can be generated by interactivity, which acts as a source of "randomness" thanks to the user's manipulation of the cursor. Reaction to the unpredictable within a given set of rules is a simplified model of the web in its entirety. Tan remarks, "Randomness provides the necessary data to set the whole process in motion. . . . I just use simple elements to represent complex and random structures. There is a certain level of randomness associated with almost all of my experiments. It's a simple way to generate values for any given system."

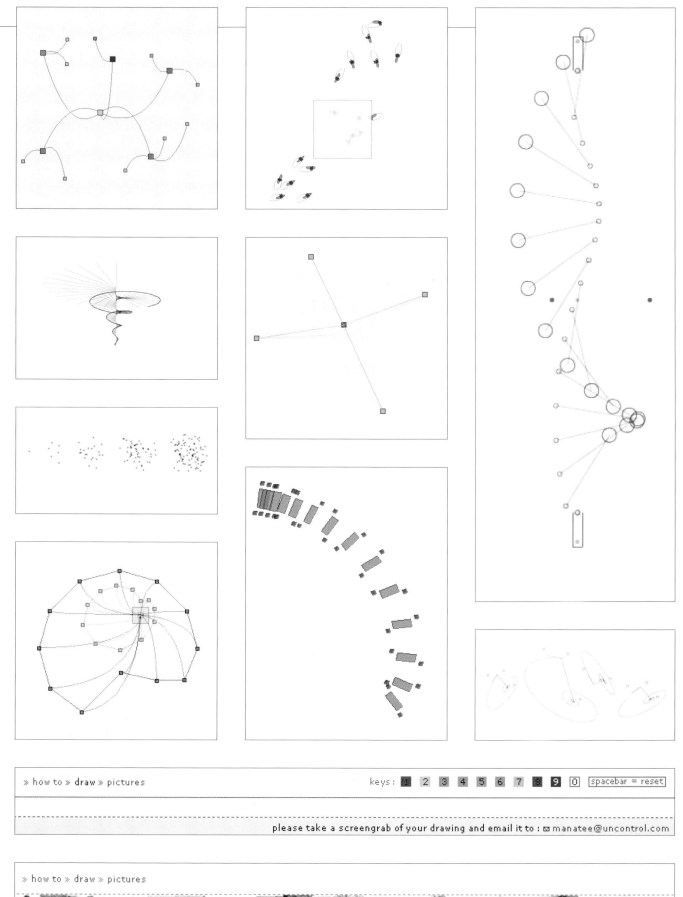

» how to » draw » pictures

keys: 1 2 3 4 5 6 7 8 9 0 spacebar = reset

please take a screengrab of your drawing and email it to : ✉ manatee@uncontrol.com

» how to » draw » pictures

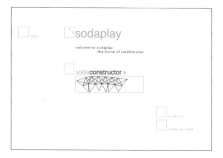

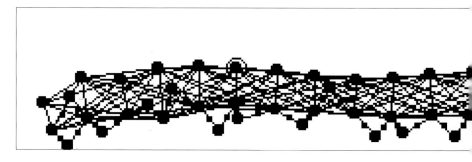

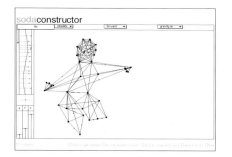

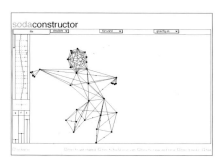

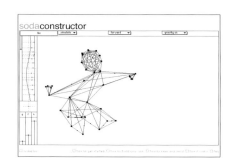

London
http://sodaplay.com
http://soda.co.uk

"The Sodaconstructor toy was originally built purely for my own amusement," writes creator Ed Burton. "I conjured it up as a fun thing to motivate me while learning the programming language Java for the first time. I never really expected anyone else would want to play with it." The flood of traffic to the Sodaplay site reached a peak of 100,000 page impressions per day soon after its appearance. As part of the Soda site, an on-line product-development group, Sodaplay is one way of joining creativity and technology. Functions such as the Sodaconstructor are familiarizing users with computer-based drawing and motion graphics. This accessibility shrinks the distance between graphics and drawing for the viewer. "I'm constantly surprised by our users," says Burton, "they're discovering ways of using Sodaconstructor that are like nothing I imagined. They're independently developing a whole genealogy of model types, some are like drawings, some are like engineering, some are just plain funny. The users are thoroughly exploring the space of possibilities in the strangely arbitrary visual medium of Sodaconstructor." The simple formulation of the Sodaconstructor and its manifestation as Burton's "bouncy dots and springy lines" rooted in a broad interest in the role of play in learning, and have led to a global community of Sodaconstructor users. There is even a virtual on-line zoo that houses contributors' bizarre creatures.

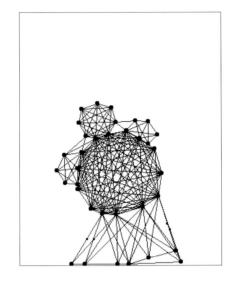

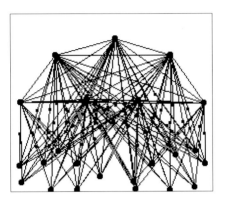

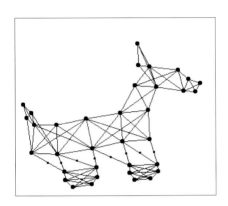

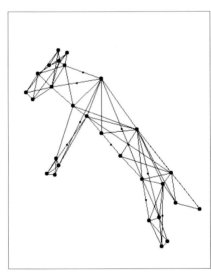

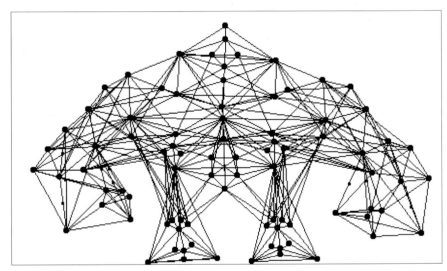

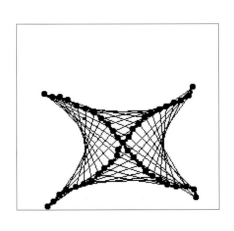

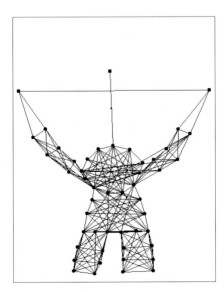

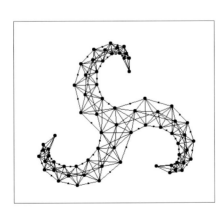

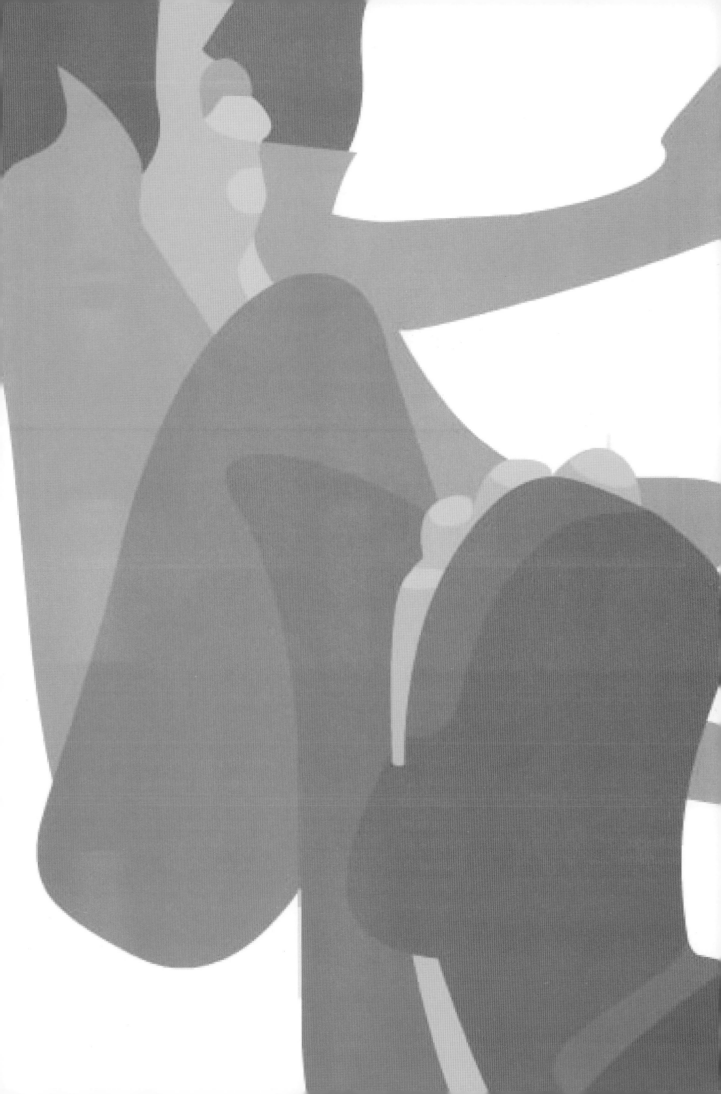

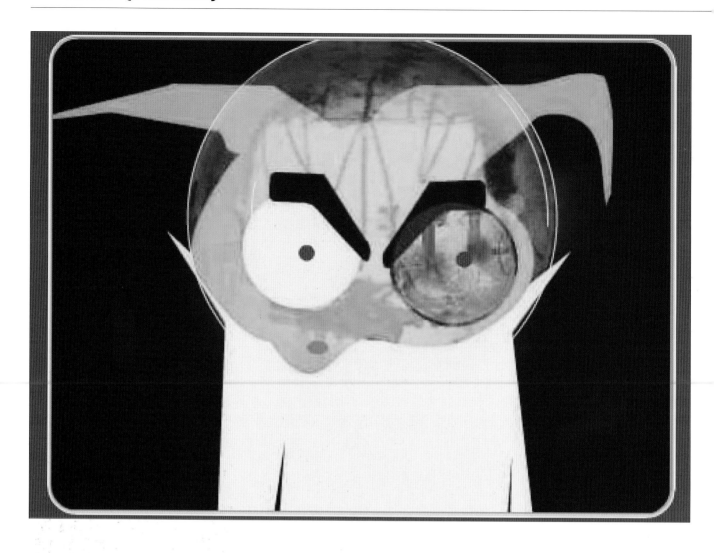

Los Angeles
www.redsmoke.com/platters

Site-creator Lew Baldwin writes, "Originally the name of my one-man band, Redsmoke was intended to be the band's site. What evolved instead was a series of animations, called 'Platters,' begun in 1997." The relative ease of producing animation with computers, as compared with labor-intensive cel animation, has opened the door for new accessibility, freedom, and experimentation with the medium. Such experimentation—wherein motion, or the mutable shape of elements, can be achieved with great economy in time and effort—is resulting in new, alternative ways of developing a story. On Redsmoke, a bizarre space creature is somehow linked with an urban gun-shootout, which then leads to a scene in an ice-cream parlor. There is also the appearance of a horned demon-cum-robot. Narrative and linear plot lines are the exception rather than the rule with many independent creations such as Redsmoke's "Platters" animation. But these new independent animations are greatly welcome, particularly as many large studios producing web animations recently seem preoccupied by the development of marketable characters and smart dialogue, and have lost a great deal of originality and innovation. This shortcoming is all the more poignant considering the possibilities afforded by the web.

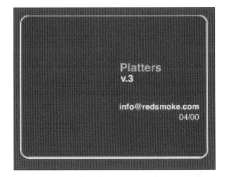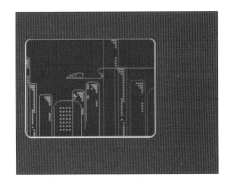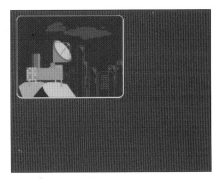
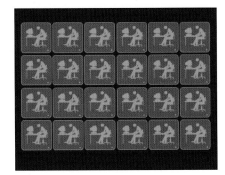
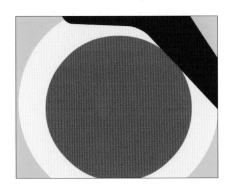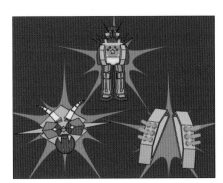
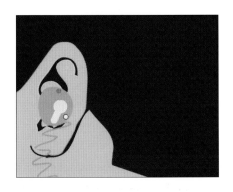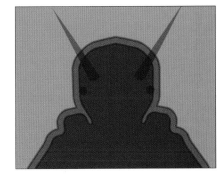
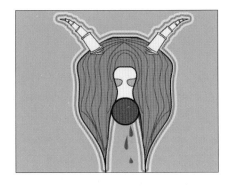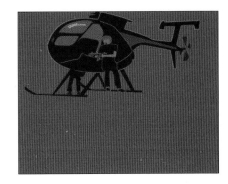

Philadelphia
www.nosepilot.com

With a logic and reasoning all its own, the world of Nosepilot unfolds in unexpected ways. A scene at the market leads to a duet of police officers, followed by the woeful drama of a girl and her pet slug. Gone is linear narrative, replaced by a play of characters in various scenes that flow uninterrupted, as in a dream. The roots of this animation are not in the web design, but in the use of Flash to give motion to the form of colors, producing a smooth stream of choreographed movement. Nosepilot is an offshoot from a larger idea of the site's creator, Al Sacui, called "El secret salami international cuisine und barber shoppe." Unlike most commercial animation typical of web broadcasting, the unformatted Nosepilot is devoid of any agenda other than its own continuation. Moreover, the format, both technical and elemental, differs from other web animations: the use of Flash as the basis for the animation provides a wholly different aesthetic—the look is lighter, pared down. The only sound in Nosepilot is music; there are no voices or sound effects. Similarly, the conception of characters is also very distinct from those of major studio productions. The continuous streaming of data in Nosepilot allows the animation to be appealingly active for the user almost immediately; this is markedly different from animations that are conceived as miniature and encapsulated movies, requiring long periods of download time.

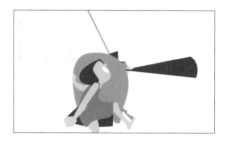

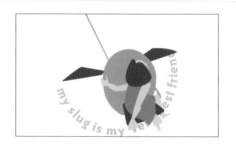

 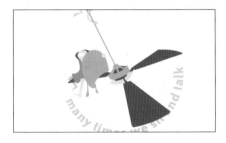 

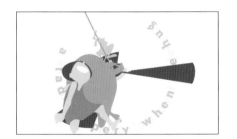 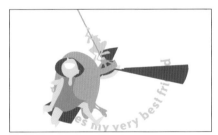 

 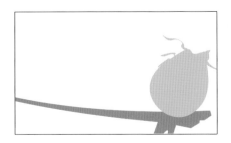 

Wellington, New Zealand
www.safeplaces.net

The serene and placid ambiance of Safeplaces has its roots in less pacific ideas, explains site-designer Toshi Endo. A singing bird named Supasta perches atop bulbous trees (reminiscent of game software) in a scenario that originally began with "atomic structures of volatile gases"—the design inspiration for the spheres in the site. What was initially planned as a venue for angst and rage, says Endo, has somehow turned into a benign pasture for relaxation and play. A sleeping boy, dreaming of re-mixing music, lies on a hillside populated by flora and fauna—a frog, fireflies, mushrooms, and the like. As the user begins to interact, he discovers a selection of music for ambient sound, a hidden passage for links and texts, and some hopping on the part of the mushrooms. Endo writes, "This is a rest stop on the web with a simple function . . . a toy I can give to people. A place you can visit where you don't have to take things so seriously . . . to chill out, take your time, and have fun." The gentle and slow movement of this site is reflected in the passage of night to day, which puts Supasta to sleep: the sky's change from light blue to deep azure, and the appearance of a crescent moon. This site provides a temporary respite on the web, which may provoke the user to ask himself, "Where is my own safeplace?"

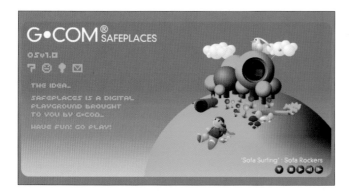

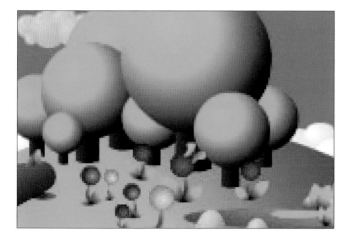

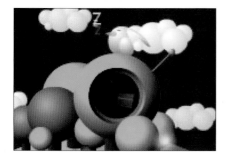

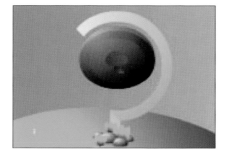

RUBBERFISH

A PVC-clad dominatrix makes her services available to a masochistic housefly. Ms. Swat (seen above) is the brainchild of Ellen McFisher, the creator of Rubberfish, an independent site for web animations and still imagery. The mixture of hand drawing with graphic structures and elements completed on the desktop makes Rubberfish simple in palette and visual organization: solid colors and clearly outlined forms. Considerations of file size and download time have influenced the aesthetic nature of the work, explains McFisher. "It is this economy that has led to my aesthetic and heightened the intensity of the style. Keeping the sound files to a minimum has also helped to create a starker visual humor, and relying less on the spoken word helps when appealing to an international audience." Despite the initial limitations presented by creating for the web, an aesthetic unto its own is germinated here. This is what has led, for example, to the convincing use of strong red and black in the Ms. Swat animations, which underscore the fetishist tone and content of the Rubberfish site.

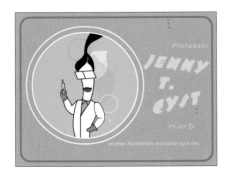

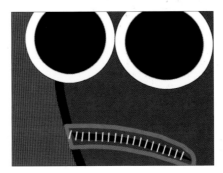

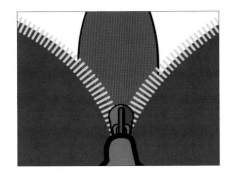

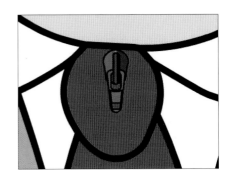

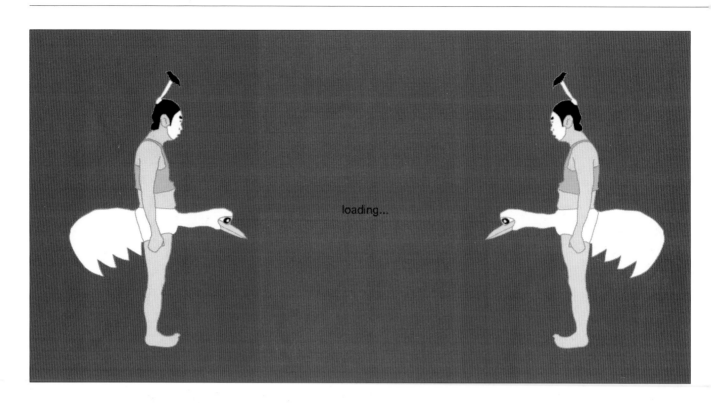

loading...

Osaka
www.i.am/otogai

Site-creator Masanori Yanagi explains that driving and dreams are the main inspirations for his bizarre Flash animations in the Otogai World gallery. In one animation, the user's cursor, scrolled over a legion of bodysuit-clad men, makes each figure repeat the same gesture (scissoring the arms back and forth before the crotch). Reducing download time for a smooth stream of moving frames has prompted some visual and stylistic basics. A limited selection of (usually solid) colors clearly separates the individual moving elements within an animation. Also, the repetition of an action or other element (either a figure or a sound) allows Yanagi to fill the screen using a minimal amount of data. Yet, as the individual components are fired in succession, in response to the user's cursor, the repetition cycles of the components are staggered. The effect is positively dream- or trancelike; this duplication of elements and the pared-down color palette help to foster the otherwordly and humorous experience of the site. Yanagi stresses that his creations cannot exist without movement and, in this regard, he feels his work is suited to the web. Beyond this, however, he feels that the extent to which the web influences the content and nature of his creations is minimal.

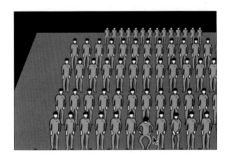

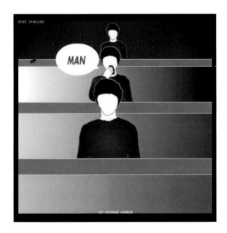

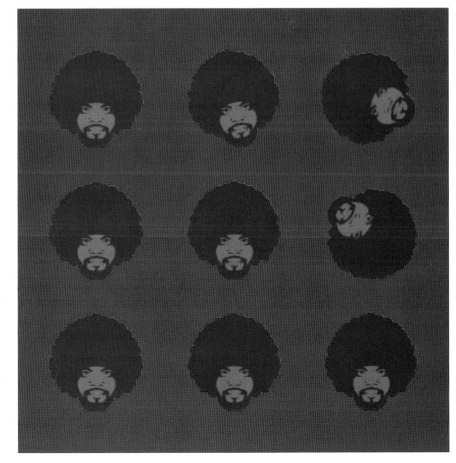

The main interface in the Rand website (created by web-design firm Rand Interactive) is a set of "three-dimensional" spheres that are put in orbit by the user's interaction. The user can zoom the perspective in and out, or revolve all of the graphic elements en masse. While the movement of the graphics in their virtual space is free and versatile, the user's own location is fixed, locked in place by a constant graphic element in the dead-center of each page, a circular silver anchor. Thus the user's sense of his own position is always clear; there is no weightless floating among the swirling colors and shapes on screen. The zoom allows the user to gain enough distance to see the extent of the graphics in a single frame; he thus has the ability to visualize the site's entire scheme in one frame, and has no need for a site map. The user's fixed location and position are used to amusing effect in the short animation "Titan Riverdance" (an anagram of the name Rand Interactive). The graphic space of the site's navigation, where the spherical objects move about, sharply contrasts to the dancing Titan, who makes his first appearance across the bottom on the site's homepage. The user, spying on the dancing Titan from a distance, is discovered. This immediately arouses the wrath of the Titan, who "attacks" the user, first pushing him onto his back (as indicated by the change in perspective) and then pulverizing him with his Riverdance stomping. The Titan then prances into the distance, leaving the user on his side, beaten.

Baltimore
www.randinteractive.com

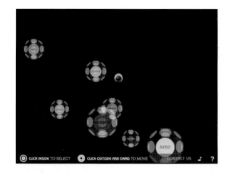

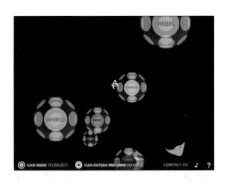

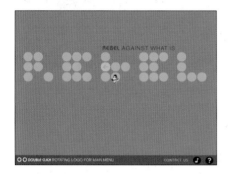
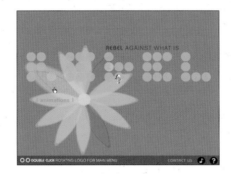
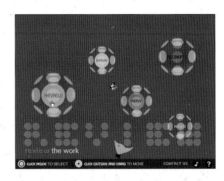

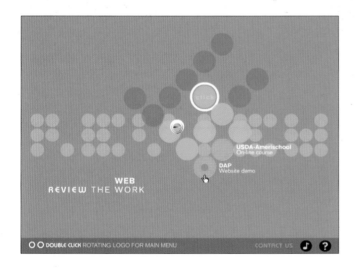
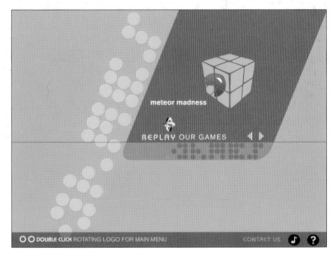

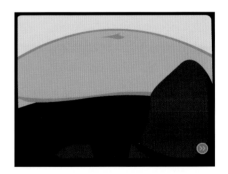

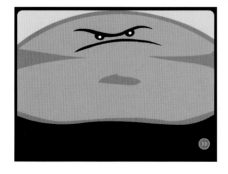

fun fun fun

has your daddy taken your t bird away?
worry not.
here are ten nice ways to have fun fun fun.

go go go to the fun fun fun

Berlin
www.flipflopflyin.com

The refined sensibility in Flip Flop Flyin's array of spectacles is reflected in the miniature size of the creator's paintbrush: a single pixel. Everything here is minute, including a collection of Pop icons and masterworks of Modern art, housed in a small-scale museum, the "Mini MoMA." But though the world is rendered here as though it is being viewed from a great distance, the emotional charge in this site is not reduced. In fact, his use of pixels as medium seems to enable the site's creator, Craig Robinson, to communicate a sense of warmth and good humor. Robinson's habit of working long nights, fueled by a steady supply of coffee, is considered in "Swimming in Coffee Boy." He succeeds in giving an emotional value to graphic elements that might otherwise remain mere specifications of data. The site provides a ten-step guide to cheering up, and a boy-meets-girl story retold as "boy-meets-pixel." (In the world of Flip Flop Flyin', it seems quite unsurprising that a boy could fall in love with a blip of color.) Even with such highly refined and developed visuals, this level of emotional response requires some significant extra element, whether simple or involved, to give a kind of life to the on-screen graphics. Robinson demonstrates one extreme for achieving such an effect.

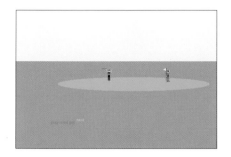

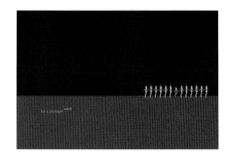

dress like elvis ^{next}

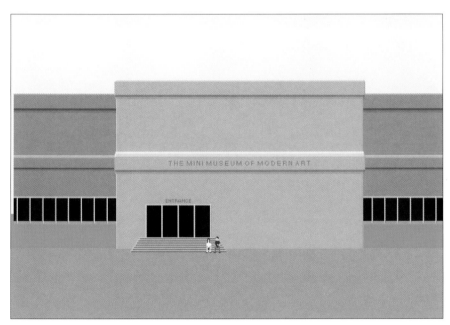

THE MINI MUSEUM OF MODERN ART

ENTRANCE

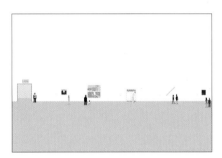

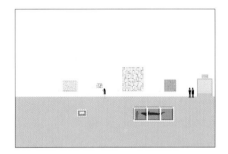

Boy Meets Pixel

starring
Meg Ryan
as Pixel

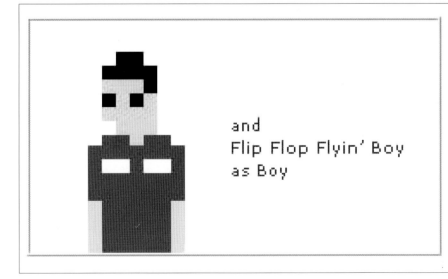

and
Flip Flop Flyin' Boy
as Boy

**SWIMMING IN COFFEE BOY
PART ONE: FREESTYLE**

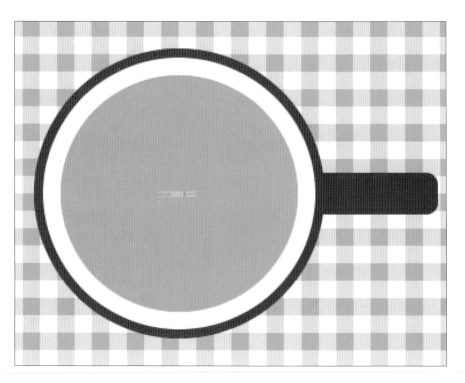

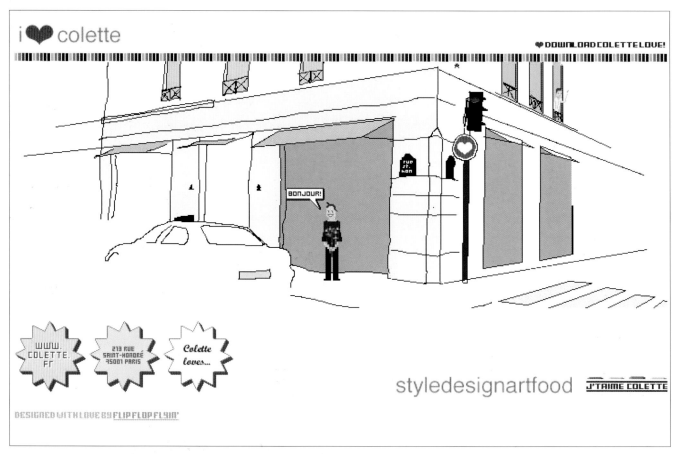

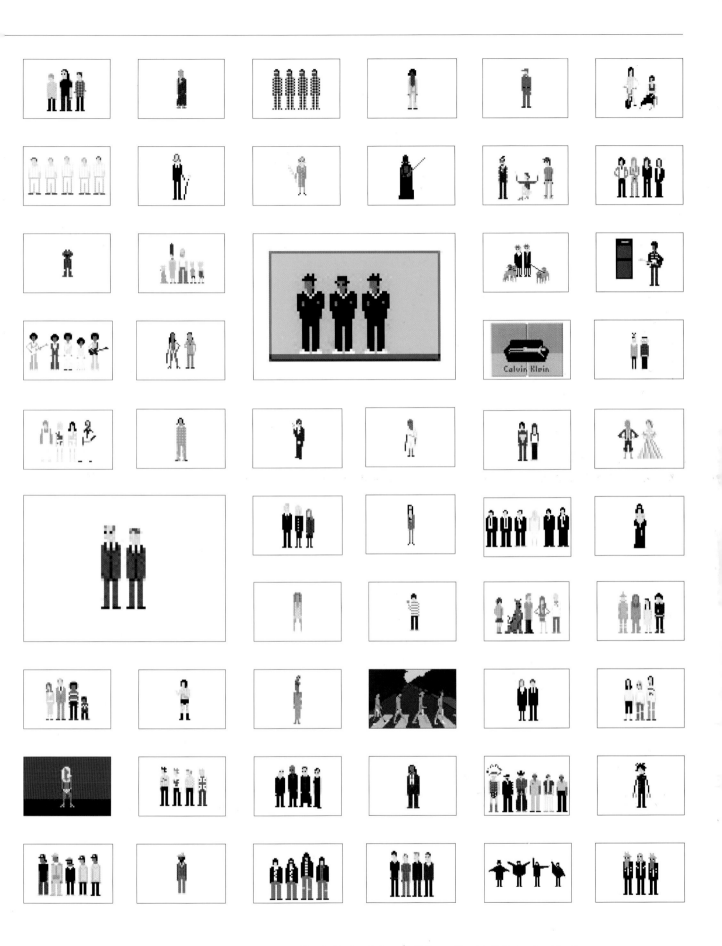

Yo La Tengo, Dalai Lama, Kraftwerk, James Brown, Fidel Castro, Cibo Matto, Beach Boys, Dali, Dame Edna, Darth Vader, Dee Lite, The Doors, Elmo, The Simpsons, Run DMC, Pet Shop Boys, Jimi Hendrix, Jackson 5, Ice T, Kate Moss, Bert & Ernie, Abba, Snoop Doggy Dog, Austin Powers, Gandhi, Mork & Mindy, King & I, Gilbert & George, Clintons, PJ Harvey, Blondie, Howard Stern, Tina Turner, Cornelius, Scoobie Doo, Wizard of Oz, Diff'rent Strokes, Andre the Giant, Erykah Badu, Red Hot Chili Peppers, X-Files, Nirvana, Lil Kim, Sex Pistols, Matrix, Reverend Al Sharpton, Village People, Edward Scissorhands, NWA, Lee Scratch Perry, Ramones, Fugazi, Beatles, and ZZ Top.

Atlanta
www.homestarrunner.com

Mike and Matt Chapman began creating and broadcasting animations using Flash after only a year of experimentation. The Chapman brothers have created a series of characters, cartoons, and games, despite their complete lack of experience in traditional cel animation. Even with the small scale of the production, this website demonstrates the new potential to create completed animation in a manner that is wholly different from traditional cel-animations. And the simple stories and cast of characters reflect the endearing naïveté of their technique. Homestar Runner, the site's armless main character, competes in a jumping-jack contest with some of the other characters: the rotund Pom Pom, the hapless Strong Sad, and Strong Bad—who in each cartoon is an incorrigible cheat. The Chapmans' earliest explorations with filmmaking date back to their childhood, playing with their father's Super 8 camera—the first technology to effectively make filmmaking an affordable hobby. Similarly, Flash and the internet now allow amateurs to create their own homemade sites. Nonetheless, even in comparison with professional studio productions of on-line animation, the quality of visuals in Homestarruner and many other small-scale sites is great. Such animations are turning out to be contenders in the larger field.

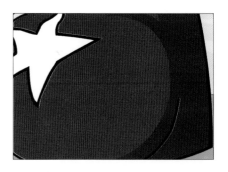

This is the King of Town

And I'm afraid a dragon has gobbled them up!

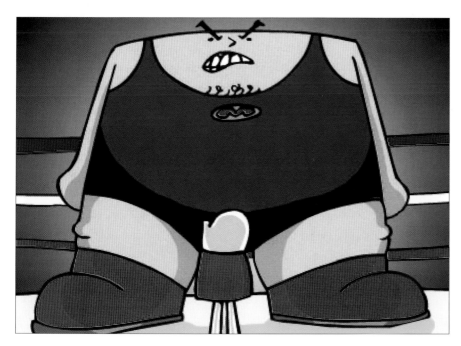

Houston
www.dementia7.com

Working for a content-development firm has helped Dementia7's creator Arik Renee Avila to understand the behavior of the web user. His greatest inspiration in designing for the internet, however, is an endless number of movies, which have influenced the decidedly entertaining quality of the site. Avila believes that building and maintaining a loyal audience requires continuous development of a site, and fidelity to the site's goals and vision. As he points out, there is little allowance for drastic changes in content—or worse, no change at all. The site must develop from project to project, but the stream of information and the navigation itself must evolve with plausible intermediary steps, not unlike a movie plot. Keeping the attention of an audience is a particular challenge in light of the age range of Dementia7's audience: 16- to 24-year-olds. For Avila, how the site evolves over an extended period is what matters most; change must happen smoothly and promote continuity. There is simply not the kind of money for on-line animation now as there is in other media; this results inevitably in less sophisticated technology and a less sophisticated look. This situation, Avila observes, is at least for the moment preventing on-line animations from evolving to the point where they can provide an experience on a par with animations in film or television.

AUDIO ON

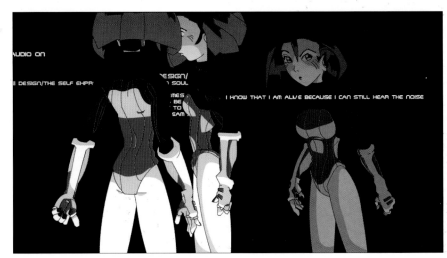

AUDIO ON

DESIGN/THE SELF EHPR

DESIGN/
SOUL

MES
BE
TO
SAM

I KNOW THAT I AM ALIVE BECAUSE I CAN STILL HEAR THE NOISE

DRAWING CG ANIME
CG?/01
character design/02
clothing design/03
character drawing/04
light and motion/05

DRAWING CG ANIME
CG?/01
character design/02
clothing design/03
character drawing/04
light and motion/05

DRAWING CG ANIME
CG?/01
character design/02
clothing design/03
character drawing/04
light and motion/05

home   BACK
prev character | next character
DRAWING CG ANIME
CG?/01
character design/02
clothing design/03
character drawing/04
light and motion/05

home   BACK
prev character | next character
DRAWING CG ANIME
CG?/01
character design/02
clothing design/03
character drawing/04
light and motion/05

Los Angeles
www.unitedbread.com

United Bread is steeped in self-styled humor. Chris Dooley, a member of the site's team of creators, describes it as "the greatest thing since sliced bread." That statement may be incidental to the true purposes of the site: to provide a forum for the creators (Saiman Chow, Brian Won, Dooley, and Sean Dougherty) to work together, and to rectify what they see as "the lack of 'us' on the web." The United Bread site supplies a series of short animations set to music. The aspect of the internet that is of greatest interest to the team is interactivity; it can, they believe, lead to an "emotional connection" between a site and its user—"the life and pulse" of that site. But the prime function of United Bread, they say, is something else altogether: "The work is extremely self-serving. We're doing it because it's funny. If something of ours makes you laugh, just know that we're laughing twice as hard, for twice as long. We are just entertaining each other." Their aesthetic sense, character design, and animations are not influenced by web graphics, they assert. Rather, their initial conception of the site was as a testing ground for the "bastard son of illustration and design." United Bread's irreverent brand of humor is particularly apparent in the character design and in a series of short films available at the site: Mao Tse Tung is outfitted with a pair of ruby-red, sparkling glasses, and James Bond is given a thick perm. The short films utilize both animation techniques and still images. The function and the direction in which this site will develop remains unclear, but the unique stamp of the creators' style represents the freedom of broadcasting on the web.

 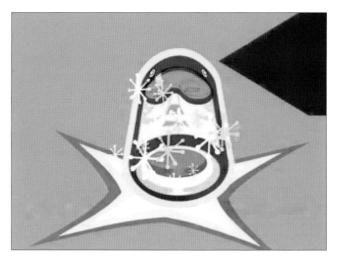

www.lessrain.com

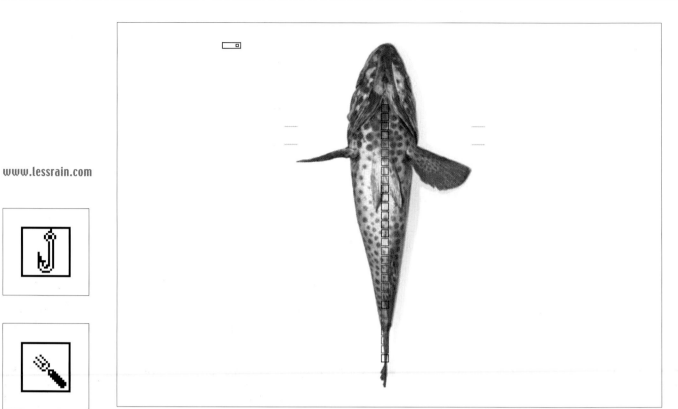

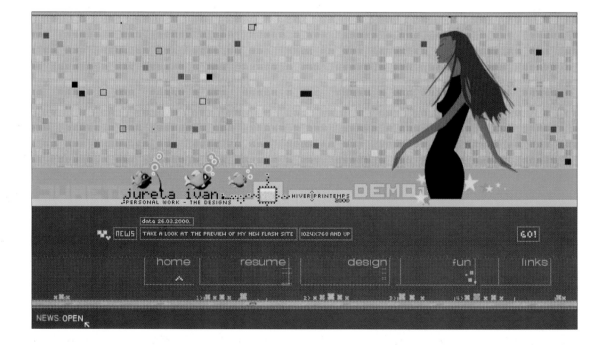

www.jureta.com

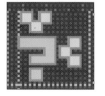

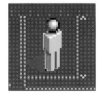

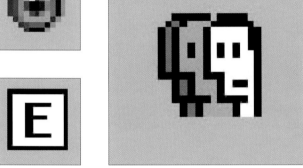

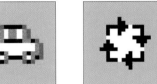

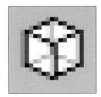

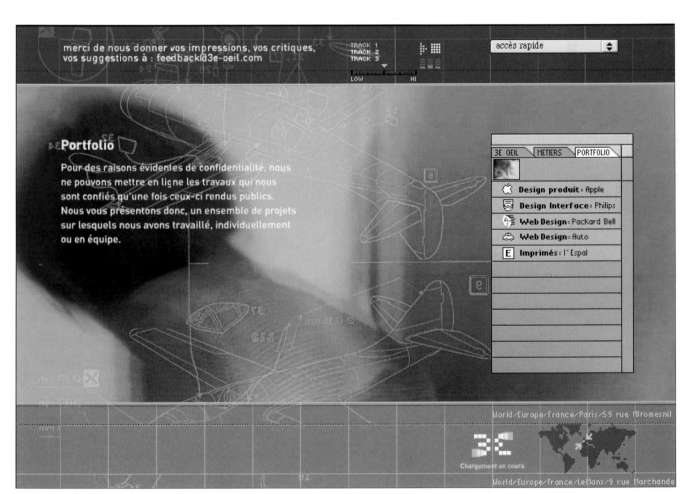

Portfolio

Pour des raisons évidentes de confidentialité, nous ne pouvons mettre en ligne les travaux qui nous sont confiés qu'une fois ceux-ci rendus publics. Nous vous présentons donc, un ensemble de projets sur lesquels nous avons travaillé, individuellement ou en équipe.

merci de nous donner vos impressions, vos critiques, vos suggestions à : feedback@3e-oeil.com

Graphic Creation, Design Interface (Philips), Design Product (Apple), Lab, Web Design (Packard Bell), Vision, Personnel, Media Interaction, Edition (l'Espal), Web Design (Auto), Method, News, Interface Design, Design Product, and Web Design.

www.3e-oeil.com

DELAWARE

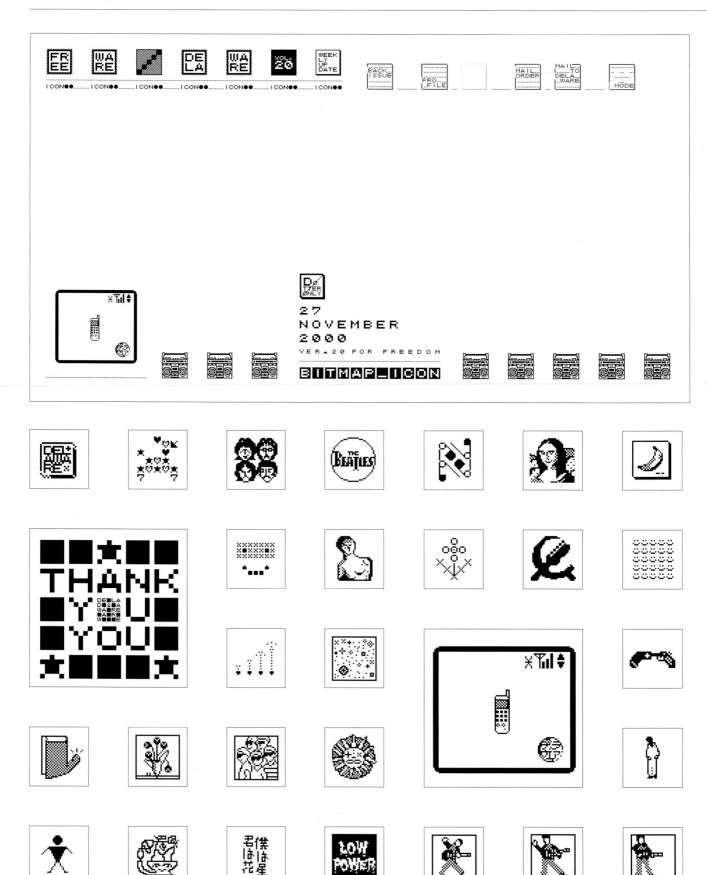

Logo, Dog, Fab Four, Beatles, Pins, Mona Lisa, Banana, Thank You, Steeler, Venus, Flower, Surfin' USSR, Smiles, Fountain, Optical, Mobile Phone, Gun & Sock; Icons by Free Delaware and Hajime Tachibana

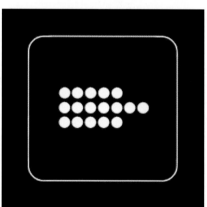

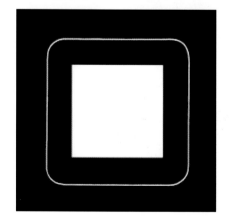

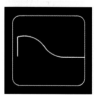

www.rhizome.net

Top page: Warhol; Duchamp, Venus, Haiku, Malevich,
International Cannibal Sign, St. Sebastien, Lascaux,
Cézanne, and Pietà.

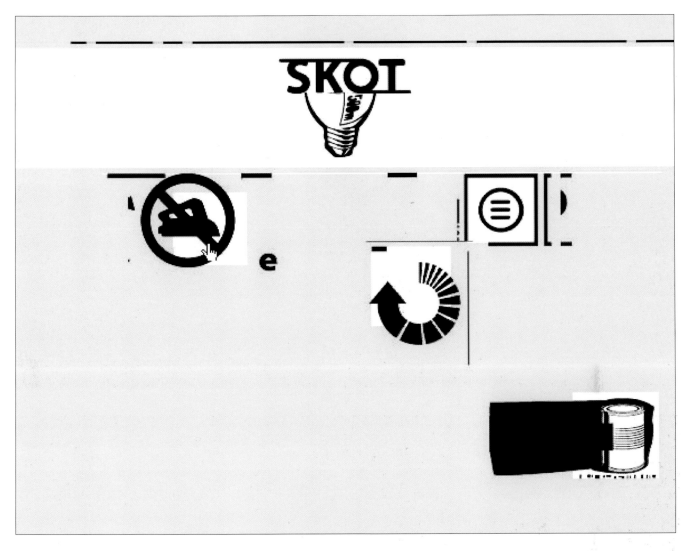

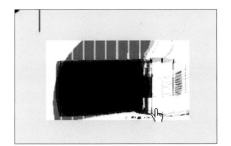
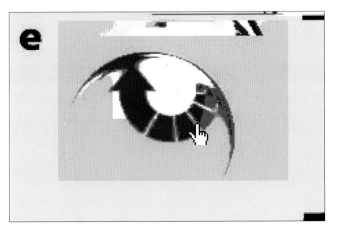

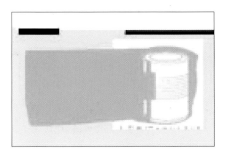

www.skot.at

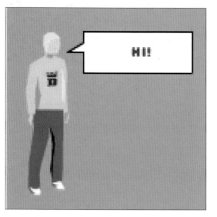

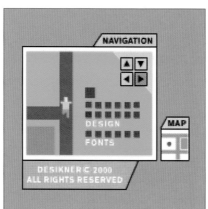

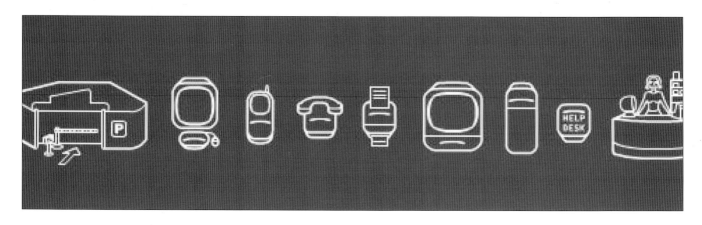

www.glassonion.com.au

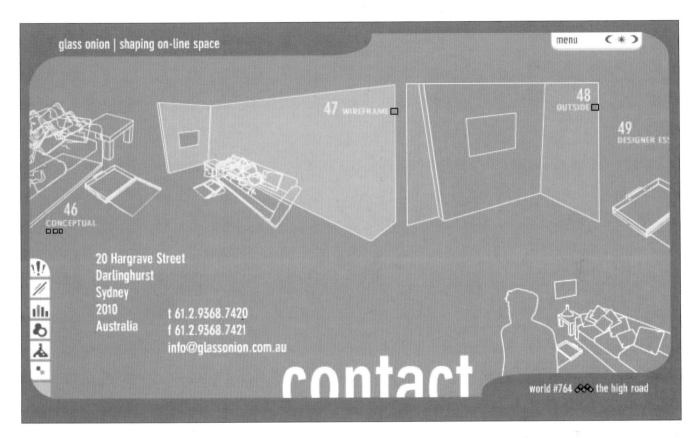

glass onion | shaping on-line space

menu

47 WIREFRAME
48 OUTSIDE
49 DESIGNER ES:
46 CONCEPTUAL

20 Hargrave Street
Darlinghurst
Sydney
2010
Australia

t 61.2.9368.7420
f 61.2.9368.7421
info@glassonion.com.au

contact

world #764 the high road

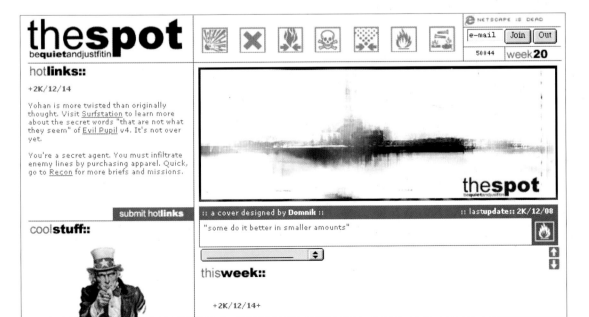

thespot
bequietandjustfitin

NETSCAPE IS DEAD

e-mail | Join | Out

50044 week20

www.thespot.com

hotlinks::

+2K/12/14

Yohan is more twisted than originally
thought. Visit Surfstation to learn more
about the secret words "that are not what
they seem" of Evil Pupil v4. It's not over
yet.

You're a secret agent. You must infiltrate
enemy lines by purchasing apparel. Quick,
go to Recon for more briefs and missions.

submit hotlinks

coolstuff::

:: a cover designed by Domnik ::   :: lastupdate:: 2K/12/08

"some do it better in smaller amounts"

thisweek::

+2K/12/14+

タクオ

アキラ

www2.airnet.ne.jp/popfly/

ヒロ

read me!

タケシ

PixelHugger
in The Field of Typography

created by pete@pixelhugger.com

〔 click to continue 〕

www.pixelhugger.com

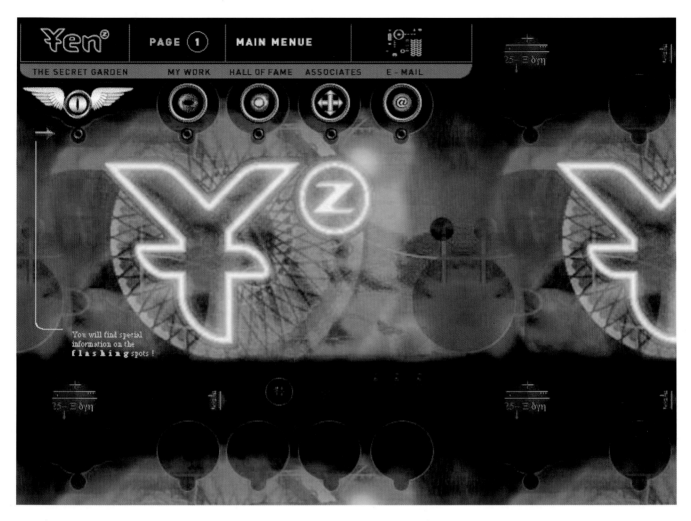

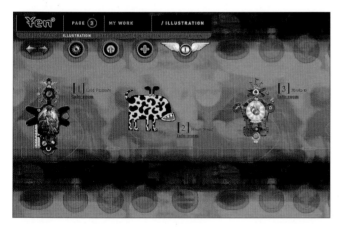

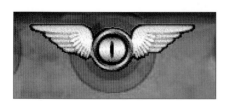

Chapter 5: Portfolio

ME COMPANY

London
www.mecompany.com

The main interface for Me Company's site is nothing more than a tunnel lined with dots. Wordless and without icons, menu, or other navigational aids, the site is designed to allow the user to explore and discover the entry and content. The navigation is strikingly simple and refined, a refreshing alternative to the whirlwind of graphics and competing elements in most websites. Me Company's senior designer Alistair Beattie describes the user's experience as "the pleasure of finding something hidden. The resulting design is one in which the interface *is* the website; there's no separation between the content and the mode of accessing that content." Exploration of the site eventually reveals a set of white dots, which link to pop-up windows that display some of the creative productions of the Me Company design firm. But rather than a mere vehicle to present the work of the studio (as a portfolio would), the site was created for the purpose of giving "presents" to its users. Thus, downloads are available in high resolution for use as desktop displays. The concept for the tunnel originated with design work Me Company created for the packaging of Björk's single "Alarm Call." The use of the individual dots as links is based on Enrico Fermi's notion of "the greatest intelligence in the smallest particles." "The dots represent a subatomic, or quantum reality," explains Beattie. "Each dot represents a potential state of visual energy; we encourage people to find this out for themselves."

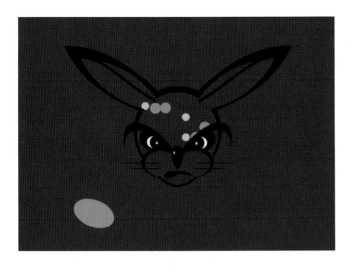

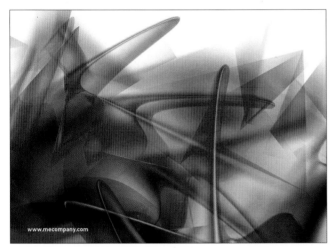

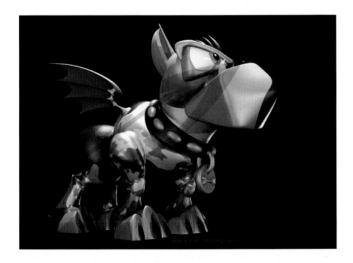
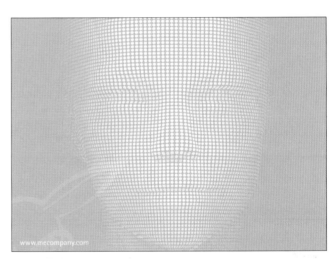

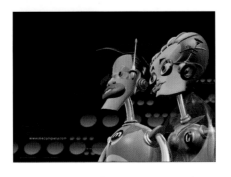
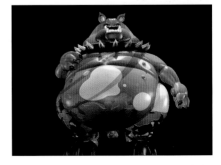

CHROMASOMA

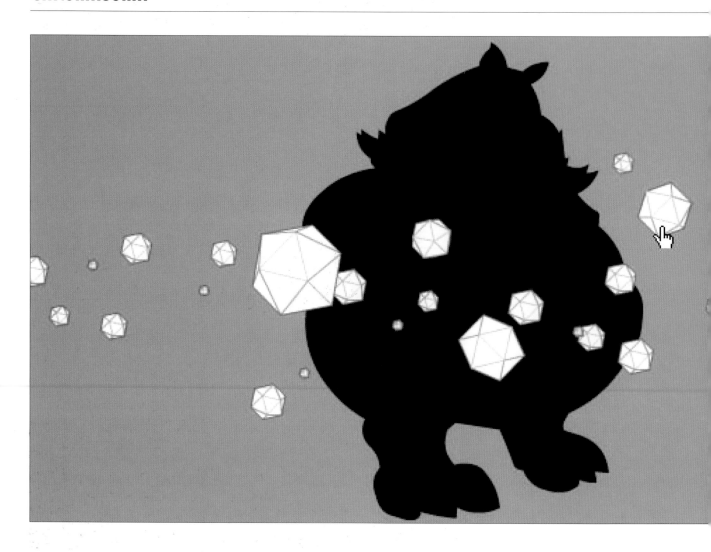

London
www.chromasoma.com

As with Me Company's site, user involvement is fundamental to the evolution and function of the site for Chromasoma, an independent character-design company born from the Me Company studio. Alistair Beattie, of Me Company, describes the themes behind the Chromasoma site as "genetic inheritance, fertilization, and fecundity." The interface presents a stream of asteroid-like kernels. The user's mouse acts to engage the "birth" of the characters, which unfurl from their cocooned slumber. As the cocoon of each character opens, through a series of cycles, text capsules that describe the character also open, while the visual data for the character itself is downloading. The total design of the site is a seamless stream of elements in which little or no time is wasted on loading data. The hybrid name Chromasoma is taken from Aldous Huxley's concept of "opiate of the masses," or *chroma* (for *chromosome*) and *soma* (for *somnolent*).

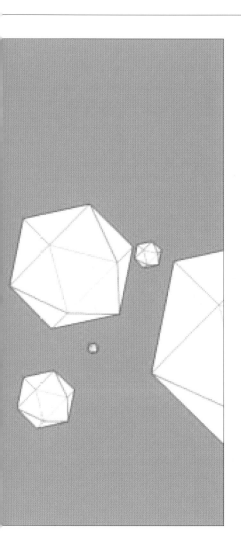

smooTHie

www.chromasoma.com

DOGSTAR

www.chromasoma.com

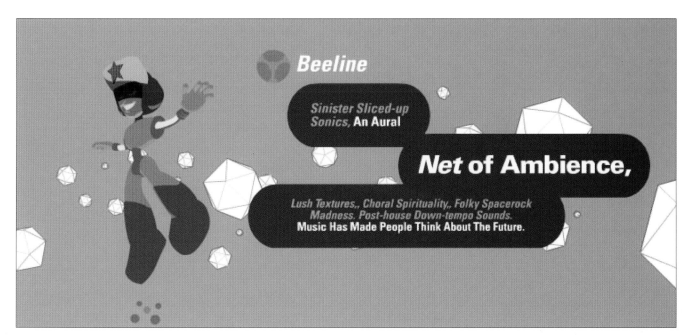

Beeline

Sinister Sliced-up
Sonics, An Aural

Net of Ambience,

Lush Textures,, Choral Spirituality,, Folky Spacerock
Madness. Post-house Down-tempo Sounds.
Music Has Made People Think About The Future.

ELIXIRSTUDIO (SUBWAY)

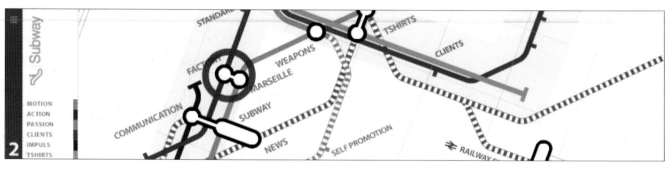

Marseille
www.elixirstudio.com

Elixir Studio is the personal site of designer Arnaud Mercier. As a laboratory of ideas for his professional work, the Elixir site has no function beyond Mercier's own explorations. Attention is focused on the developments of autonomous graphics and on navigation as a function of its presentation. Elixir Studio is split into two separate interfaces: "Subway" and "UP." In "Subway," there is a zoom feature that allows a scaled-back perspective of the map, showing the total extent and organization of the site. The user is constantly aware of his own relative location. The literal use of the familiar subway map as a motif makes for easy recognition and retention in the user's memory. The utility of the subway is a poignant metaphor here. As Mercier remarks, design is for communication and functionality as well as aesthetics. "You have to think about design with the dimension of time, like a movie; and more: you have to think about the user's experience."

2 | NUMERO NEUF
OFFICE DE LA CULTURE DE MARSEILLE
GRAPHIK ID. V 2

Numero Neuf

1 | Airport

elixirstudio 2

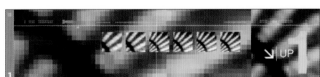

UP 1

3 | Cook

Graphik Brain + *Hot Graphik Salsa*

2 | Ftw98

Pirate
2

PIRATE
SELF PROMOTION
3D MODELING

UP

New York
www.no-sleep.com

Sound, photography, calligraphy, graffiti-inspired lettering, and new web graphics all come together in the No Sleep site. Functioning sometimes as a portfolio for the designer Arnold Marzan, and at other times as his creative outlet, the site has a very simple structure. A scrolling menu that appears and disappears in the center of the screen is decidedly subtle; there is no complex or intricate interactivity here. Similarly, trends in web design and graphics are rejected in favor of influences that have particular (if sometimes oblique) meaning for Marzan: "Kids eating ice cream, dog parks, panhandling bums on the street, riding the subway late nights, DVDs, graff burners, throw-ups, can control, upward fades, Japanese commercials, eighties monster rock ballads, old Latin freestyle, New Wave, turntables, cross-faders with contour control, crabs, flares, chirps, beat juggles, random daily commuters, crayons, tourists, citywide construction, fashion, toys, letters from Mom, museums, advertisements, park squirrels coming up to you asking for a cigarette, sidewalk shish-kebab vendors, nuts for nuts, 'Buy her a flower?,' $20 lapdances, sugared-up beers in Madison Square Garden, multinational superconglomerates, clouds that look like bunny rabbits that got their heads cut off, Keroppi, Iceberg Slim, whatever, whenever, anything, everything."

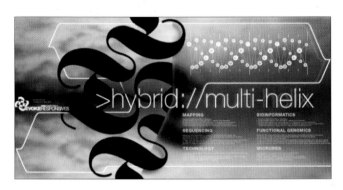

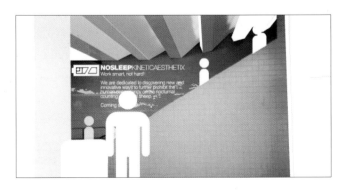

✓ SECOND CROP
01 ‹
02 ‹

*

"WHEN SOMEONE SAYS INTERACTIVE TELEVISION >
THINK INACTIVE HUMANS"
- SUEELLEN - NUMERO 1 - SLAP OF REALITY

AS A FEW OF YOU WILL KNOW, DESIGN, WHEN IT IS THE ARTICULATION OF THE
ARTISTIC AND THE INTELLECTUAL, THE IDEOLOGICAL AND THE SPIRITUAL, THE
MUNDANE AND THE TRANSCENDENT, THE BEAUTIFUL AND THE AFFECTING, IS
A POWERFUL TOOL MORE THAN THAT, IT IS, OR CAN BE, A GIFT.

IF YOU NEED ME TO COMPLETE THAT THOUGHT, GO AWAY.

WE ARE NOT GOING TO GLOSS THIS, OR MARKET IT, OR AESTHETICISE IT AS
'CULTURE-JAMMING'.
WE ARE NOT GOING TO SPELL OUT YOUR RESPONSIBILITIES TO YOU.
WE ARE NOT GOING TO JUSTIFY YOUR PRESUPPOSITIONS.
WE ARE NOT GOING TO LEND CREDIBILITY TO YOUR CULTURAL INDEX.
WE ARE NOT GOING TO FACILITATE YOUR PASSIVITY, OR GLORIFY ACQUIESENCE
WE ARE NOT GOING TO BE PLEASANT.
WE ARE NOT GOING TO BE ACCOMODATING.

AND YES, WE ARE TALKING TO YOU.
DON'T CONCERN YOURSELF WITH WHETHER OR NOT WE KNOW WHO YOU ARE
TRY TO FIGURE OUT WHO WE'RE TALKING TO INSTEAD. THAT'LL BE A START.

WE WILL OFTEN BE UNNATTRACTIVE
WE WILL OCCASIONALLY BE UNINTERESTING.
WE WILL OFTEN BE UNINTELLIGIBLE
WE WILL OCCASIONALLY BE PRETENTIOUS -

YOU HAVE NO REASON FOR BEING HERE UNLESS YOU ARE LOOKING FOR
SOMETHING.

DO NOT DRIFT AIMLESSLY FROM ONE AIMLESS COLLECTION OF AIMLESSNESS
TO ANOTHER.
PLEASE, QUESTION THIS EVEN AS YOU ASK YOURSELF WHY YOU SHOULD BE
QUESTIONING IT.
QUESTION WHY YOU SHOULD BE QUESTIONING.

AND WHEN YOU FINALLY SPEAK, HAVE SOMETHING TO SAY. WE DO.

In response to the prevalence of what Submethod's creators call the "empty narratives and technical tricks" broadcast on the web, they have worked collectively to produce a site with some depth of emotion and thought. Mike Young's initial intention was to create a site that would be interdisciplinary, involving music, filmmaking, design, and writing. He invited others working in the web industry—Stanley Wolukau-Wanambwa, Sean Foyle, and the group known as the Nineteen Point Five Collective (NPFC)—to collaborate on the site, which has come to serve as an on-line gallery for their own digital artwork. The site was created to "express personal things in compelling, unique, and resonant ways." The work is assembled and "exhibited" only on the web as the contributors are based in four different cities: London, Washington D.C., Los Angeles, and Detroit. "It is the core component of the creativity that ultimately resides on the screen," say the site's creators. "Mike's graphic imagery, photography, and compositions evoke particular intellectual and emotional responses from Stanley as a writer, and from Sean as a 3D artist. Music from NPFC collides and converges with certain visual and semantic currents in the design, or provides the foundation for different ideas that are then passed around the collective digitally." The themes and topics of their productions are personal, ranging from love to the pain of watching a friend plagued with drug addiction. As the creators themselves admit, what has been accomplished thus far is only a start when compared to the potential of the medium. But Submethod demonstrates that content developed in direct response to the nature of the medium itself can be most effective.

www.submethod.com

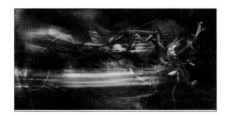
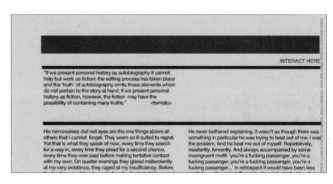

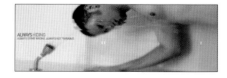

FUTUREFARMERS

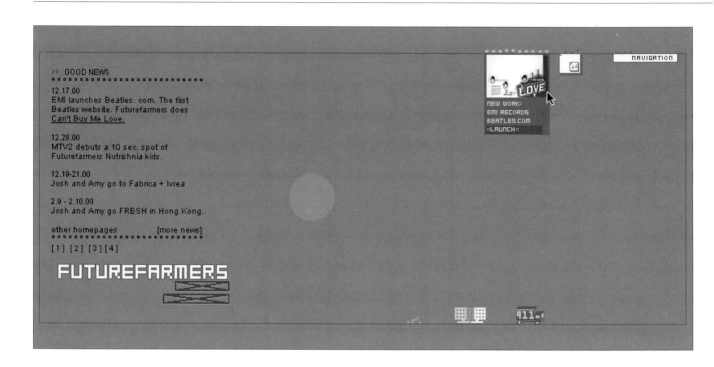

Founded by designer Amy Franceschini, Futurefarmers was launched primarily as an experimental playground for her design work. Though the site continues to serve her design studio in this capacity, it has since grown into a communal venue. Additionally, it has social and political functions: the Futurefarmers site disseminates information about technology and agriculture. During the war in Kosovo, Futurefarmers broadcast "Kosovo Elf," a game for saving Albanians. "The work I have done on the web has influenced the way I think about things in terms of social, political, and community relations. It has made me look at networked systems, which has been most influential. The user contribution available on Futurefarmers has not influenced our sense of design. Rather, it has informed us who our users are and how they think in a given situation. It has inspired us to do more applications where users are more a part of the site." The site's drive to involve users is about connecting people to one another, as opposed to connecting users to the machine. As Franceschini explains, the paragon of true interactivity is nature, as opposed to "techno-fetishism." Her concept of organizing physical spaces in terms of a network of systems has provided part of the agenda for the site. In fact, the name "Futurefarmers" derives from Franceschini's own goal of creating an actual "farm," she says, "where we continue to work on our art and design, and also facilitate other artists with space and a place to share ideas."

San Francisco
www.futurefarmers.com

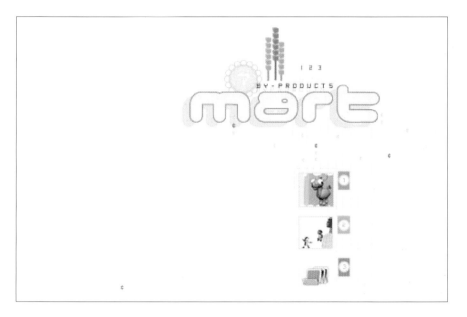

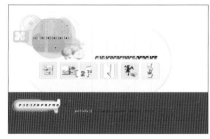

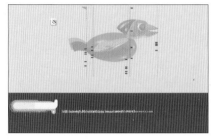

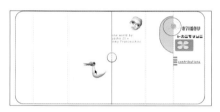

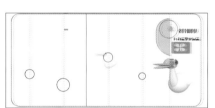

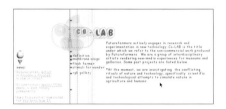

FUTUREFARMERS: CULTIVATING YOUR CONSCIOUSNESS

05.19.00
Sascha Merg and Amy
Franceschini in Sapporo,
Japan. Sumo is truely an in-
spiration. Point your browsers
to www.shift.jp.org for cover!!

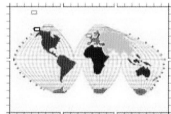

::>>>>::DEVELOP:::::::::::::::::::::::::::::::::::::::
:::COMMUNICULTURE::::::::::::::::::::::::::::::::::::
----
old homepage archive: <u>1</u>   <u>2</u>   <u>3</u>

>>F u t u r e f a r m e r s>>cultivating your consciousness:: 1201 howard street. suite B.
San Francisco. CA 94103   ph. 415.552.2124 fx 626.8953 email <u>ame@sirius.com</u>

as always... sound by <u>airking</u>

Recent clients: Swatch, Adobe, Shift Productions, Webby's. See the rest in the
<u>informative</u> section of our site.

EXPERIENTIAL

INFORMATIVE

PRODUCTS
++

Since 1997, we have hosted 6 artists +
developed experimental and client
projects together. (See co-lab section
for more info) Please welcome our
newest residents:

Karen Hansen:Denmark: <u>Space Invaders</u>
<u>Martina Hofflin</u>: Germany
Justin Bakse: Minneapolis: <u>MCAD</u>
+++

***x * *SILO** *

++ <u>Download Silo</u>
Silo sits on your desktop. It automatically
updates latest Futurefarmers information
and a running list of our favorite urls
without launching any browsers.

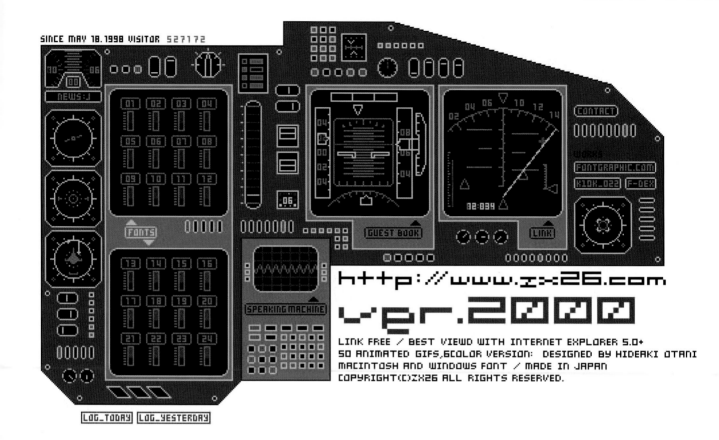

Tokyo
www.zx26.com
www.fontgraphic.com

ZX26 is web-designer Hideaki Ootani's site for free fonts, while www.fontgraphic.com presents Ootani's fonts for sale. Fontgraphic also has its own 'zine, *f-dex* (also available for free in print version, distributed in Tokyo). The site's initial inspiration came from the control panel of a Boeing 747, in which gauges and needles fluctuate. Ootani found this attention to small movements of tiny graphic elements fascinating, and has successfully worked with this idea on his website. Here, the play of needles on meters swinging and the undulation of gauges are simulated with the animation of dots. The use of graphic miniaturization seems limitless, as legibility continues to achieve greater levels of refinement. Individual meters and gauges operate independently within a larger structure (as in an airplane's control panel); the entire website is thus consolidated into one unified interface, which serves as both content and navigational tool.

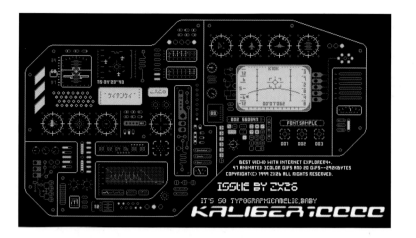

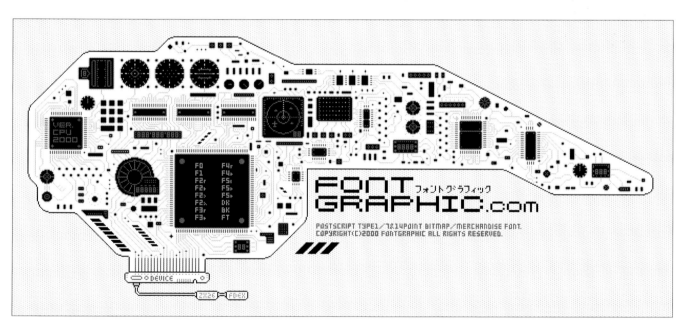

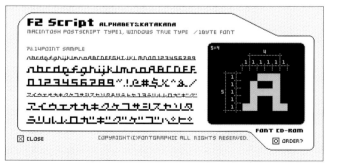

KALIBER 10000

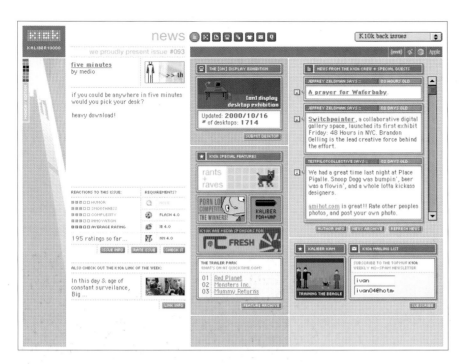

Kaliber 10000, or K10K is a site where designers and web creators can exchange ideas and thoughts. Created by the Danish team of Mschmidt, Token, and Per, as a purely design-oriented and design-driven site, K10K is a natural magnet for creators of all genres working on the web. The number of daily hits from this sophisticated audience indicates that K10K has a large community of users—most of whom are probably accustomed to tiny graphics and fine print like those used on the site. K10K offers a weekly "front page," with news stories on design written by a stable of contributing authors, as well as a section called "Issues," devoted to showcasing work by various creators (individuals or entire design studios) who have been invited to contribute. Keeping the site fresh and constantly developing new material for posting is now the main focus of K10K. Mschmidt observes: "Both Token and I get bored extremely fast—we truly are products of the 20-second-attention-span generation. So our main priority when designing K10K was to make sure that everything was tiny, very tight—but with a lot of stuff going on. That way the website would keep on being fresh and interesting, even for the two of us who spend a lot of time on the site every day." This mania for constant change and innovation is also fueled by the excitement of working in a field that is still quite new, still in many ways undefined. This is a medium that is in the process of discovering its own form and "rules"; the state of flux is enough to make web designers "schizophrenic," writes Mschmidt. "It is so funny that everybody tries to establish some sort of code of honor, rules of what is good and bad . . . and not just accepting that this is the very first step in a direction that you will never be able to foresee. We are all alone. It is beautiful and a bit scary (like in monster-under-the-bed scary)."

London and Copenhagen
www.k10k.net

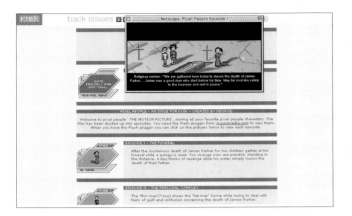

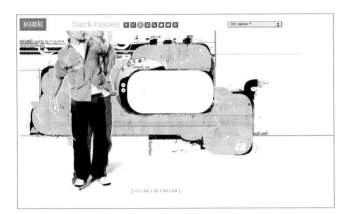

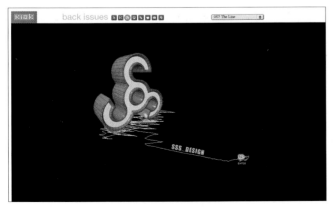

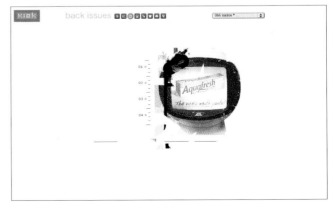

San Francisco
www.ndroid.com

The long graphic-cityscape scroll across the screen at the nDroid site takes its inspiration from the Copenhagen skyline. Each house serves as a compartment for one of the different sections of the site, which range in function and content: quizzical texts, downloads for cutout characters, a game of connect-the-dots, and a short film about cats. The air of domesticity sets the mood for the prime function of the site: a portal for drawing. The site's creator, Vicki Wong, considers herself a "compulsive drawer" and uses nDroid as a collective portfolio for people with the same penchant for the medium (users may post their own contributions in the site). There are several regular contributors who occupy their own private virtual lots within the site. They scan their flat art and submit the material for posting. The graphics of the site are inspired by a 'zine self-published by Wong in the eighties. The clip-art decorations, patterns, and borders of the paper-and-glue 'zine have found a new home in the nDroid site.

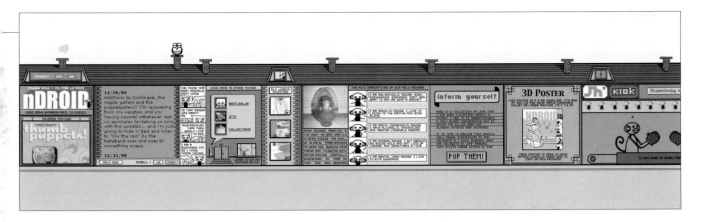

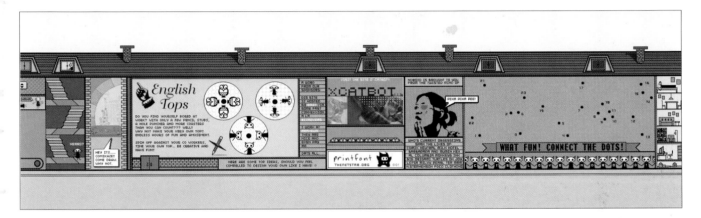

COLOURED PUPPETS

Faery Beary
Baloo Bunny
Katatonic
Frogga
Space Gerbil
Mightee Munki
Mus Mus
Pandalicious

B&W PUPPETS
[COLOUR YOURSELF!]

Faery Beary
Baloo Bunny
Katatonic
Frogga
Space Gerbil
Mightee Munki
Mus Mus
Pandalicious

PUPPET GALLERY

Send in a photo
of you with your
favorite puppet!!

NDROID PRESENTS

thumb
puppets!

SPACE GERBIL
download hi-res : space.pdf : 231k

Instructions: Download. Print. Cut along dotted line. Cut
out mouth hole. Stick thumb through. Have fun!! (nDroid
is not responsible for any injuries or paper cuts obtained
while enjoying our fine products.)

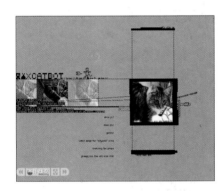

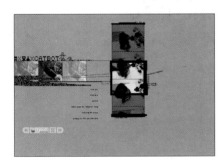

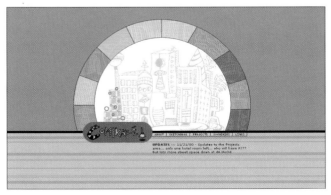

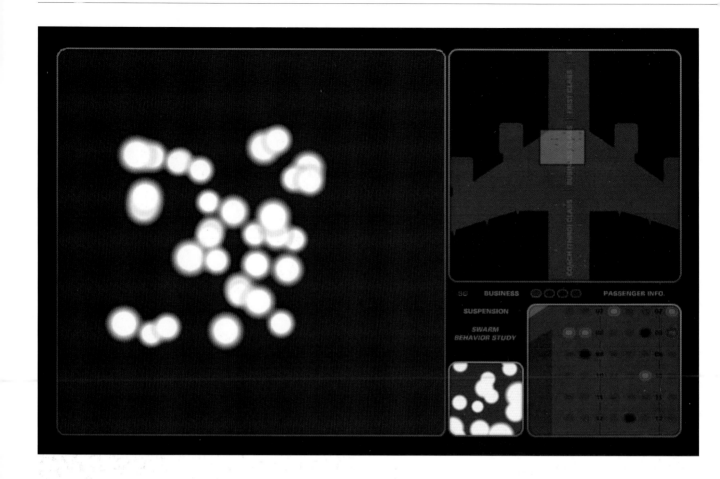

Boston
www.flight404.com

The fictional Flight 404 was originally intended to have crashed, according to the site's creator, Roger Hodgin. He had planned to create an homage to the imaginary plane wreck, but this narrative has been lost. What remains is the use of the virtual flight with passenger seating arrangements as the site's interface. The passengers in the different sections of the fuselage and the crew in the cockpit function, in fact, as action-script experiments. Hodgin had created a host of small Flash experiments and wanted to present them in a manner other than small-sized thumbnail reproductions. Mass-transit signage has been a source of inspiration for Hodgin, and when developing the interface of the Flight 404 site, he decided to use a streamlined, icon-like style characteristic of signs at airports. Of his web-design work, Hodgin writes, "The largest realization that I have come to is that I will never be satisfied. I think this is a problem that plagues *all* designers, but . . . web designers feel this all the more intensely. There are so many beautiful and inspiring presentations on the internet, it's hard to get through a project without wanting to change the look entirely before the project is completed."

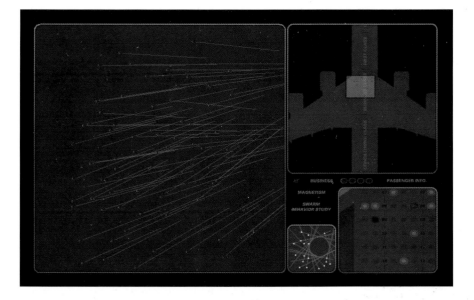

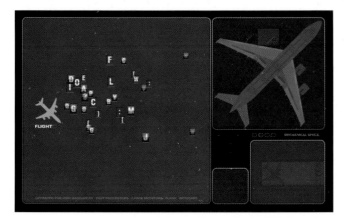

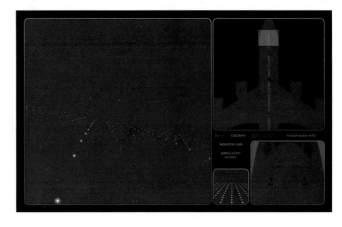

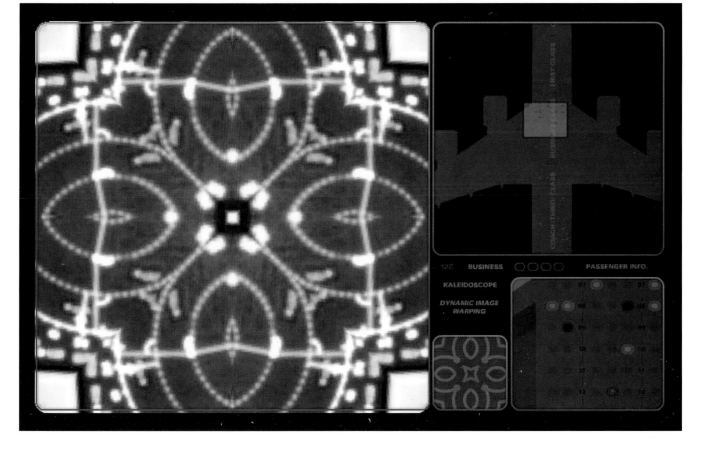

London & Tokyo
www.plusism.com

Duo Matius Gerardo Grieck and Tsuyoshi Nakazako work in various media, usually with topics and themes that are multiple in form, function, and production. Their work has involved a range of production genres, among them installation art and experimental film. Their +ISM website is interdisciplinary, and includes a font design, a section of still images assembled in a gallery called "Neutrons," and a "Synthetic Environment" that is an amalgam of digital imagery and virtual spaces. Grieck and Nakazako hold that "the site itself is treated as a mere stage, and is used as a venue for digital artwork and to escape the trappings of analog physicality." Nonetheless, this "stage" is set with an array of graphics and links that make the navigation of the site itself a pleasure. But the creators maintain that these devices are meant to lure the user into the different levels of their site—a sort of aesthetic ambush. "It is the 'bait' we use to let you believe that what you see is 'sincere,' but there is only uncertainty and a general loss of references/values; a construction of models that create what we experience as so-called 'reality.' Once the definition of opposites is neutralized, there is no distinction left between opposing values such as authentic-false, real-unreal, honest-dishonest etc." This dissolution of dualities also allows for multiple approaches to the content of the site. Yes-no prompts, menus, and other trademark signs of smooth and controlled navigation are nowhere to be found. What's more, a scramble of overlaid texts (as on the facing page) can be read in parts and in any order. In all, the site results in being obscure and elliptical in a straightforward fashion.

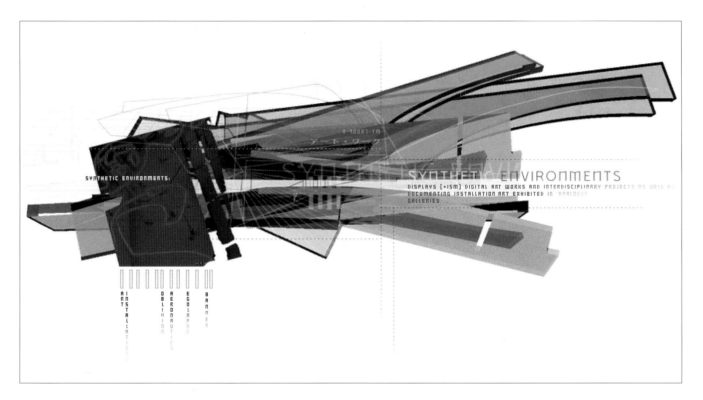

SYNTHETIC ENVIRONMENTS:

SYNTHETIC ENVIRONMENTS
DISPLAYS [+ISM] DIGITAL ART WORKS AND INTERDISCIPLINARY PROJECTS AS WELL AS DOCUMENTING INSTALLATION ART EXHIBITED IN ANALOGUE GALLERIES

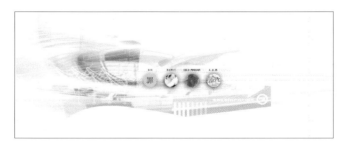

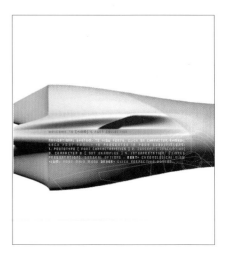

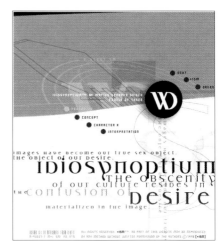

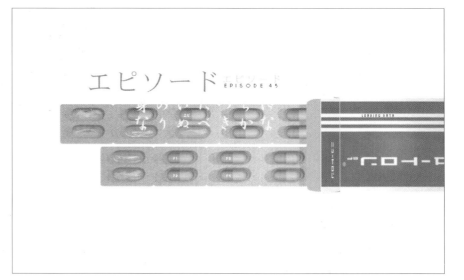

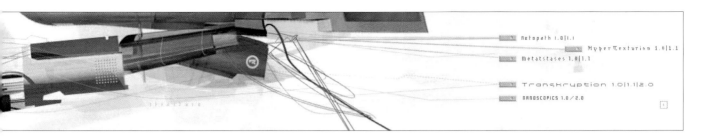

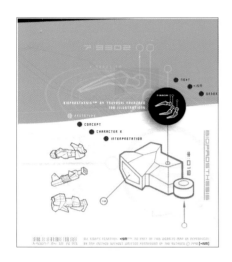

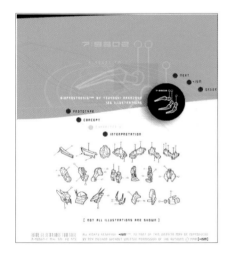

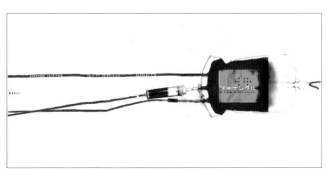

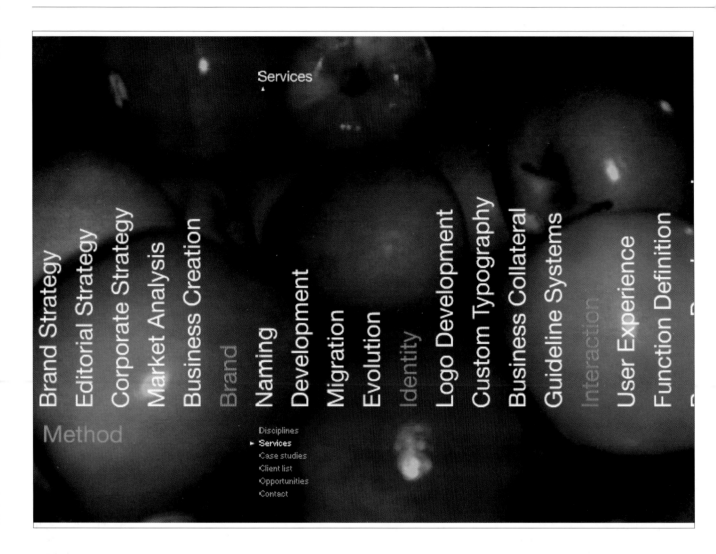

New York
www.method.com

The Apartment was designed as a new type of shopping experience, intended to appeal to a hip market in New York's downtown area. The "apartment" itself is a furniture and life-style store housed within an actual New York apartment—a place of business by day, and a home during the off-hours. Periodically, the store is moved to a new apartment locale, with an entirely new stock of merchandise. Information about the shop's whereabouts can be accessed through the website, which was created by design firm Method. Along with the Apartment, Method has designed other sites for several commercial clients. Their research endeavors have prompted the team to create an auxiliary section to their own site—the "3d Engine"—in order to develop and experiment with various web-design techniques. As designer Jonathan Snyder explains, the goal of the "3d Engine" is "to create an innovative approach to the display of information about the individual experiments in the lab. The challenge was to design an interaction system with an architecture that was not predetermined. In this system, information related to individual experiments—such as author, type of experiment, creation date—could be sorted and presented in any number of ways, depending on how users interacted with the site."

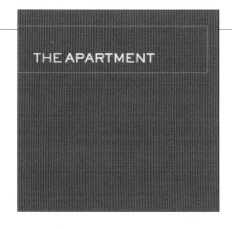

THE APARTMENT

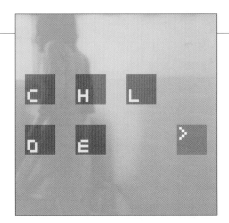

C H L
O E >

I saw this daybed a couple of days after I met Peter for the first time. I thought this might be the right thing to have if I'm going to invite him over sometime – so I got it. When he finally came over, I realized I'm more comfortable with my new daybed than with Peter.

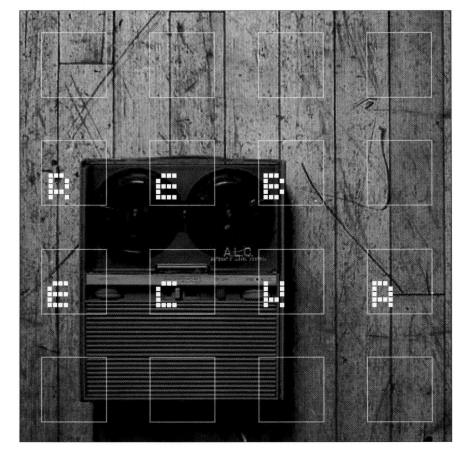

R E B
E C R
A

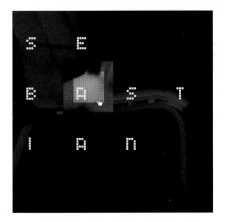

I honestly do not remember much about my date with Chloe. Only that she really seemed to be a dreamer - a romantic. It didn't go too well for me ... what can I say.

S E
B S T
I A N

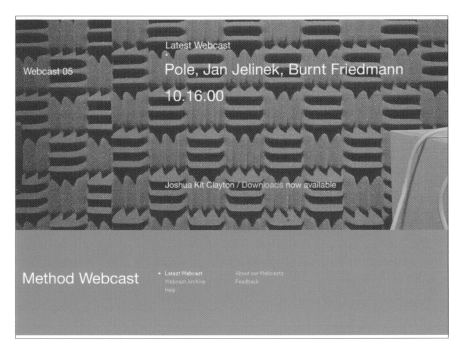

Webcast 05

Latest Webcast

Pole, Jan Jelinek, Burnt Friedmann

10.16.00

Joshua Kit Clayton / Downloads now available

Method Webcast · Latest Webcast   About our Webcasts
                 Webcast Archive   Feedback
                 Help

Webcast Archive
Select Cast
01   02   03   04
05   06   07   08
09   10   11   12
13   14   15   16

Method Webcast

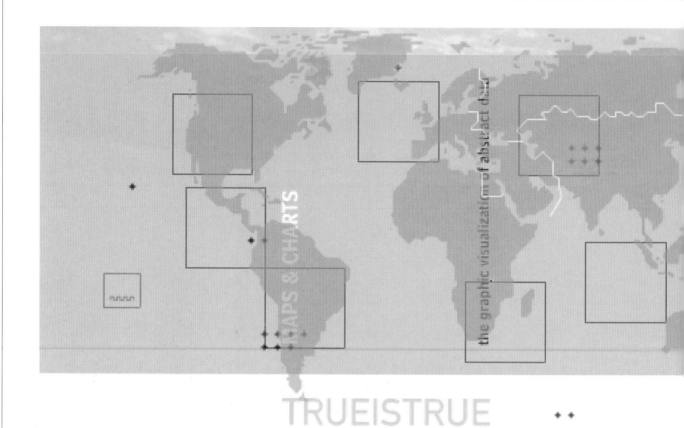

Minneapolis
www.trueistrue.com

Motion graphics aren't just about high-speed action. Though Michael Cina, the creator of Trueistrue, uses Flash, he is very critical of its overuse and of animated graphics that he feels lack depth of meaning. Cina has created work that is difficult to describe in terms of conventional contemporary website design. There are no pop-up boxes, hyperlinks, or scrolling text; in fact, there is no navigation of any kind. The extent of the site is a single main page, which is periodically replaced by an entirely new creation. The main page (pictured here) consists of graphic elements in a state of slow and steady evolution. Graphic elements and sounds phase in and out in a graded sequence. Compared to the blur of moving graphics common to most websites, the pace of change in this site is as calm as the change from day to night. "Much of Flash use is meant for instant gratification," says Cina. "It seems so automated and fake. One of my main goals for the site is to challenge web animation and how people view the web. The web has been seen as a resource and a breeding ground for consumerism for far too long. I want to change that and make the viewer *think*. But since my early animations were very slow, a lot of users had no idea what was going on."

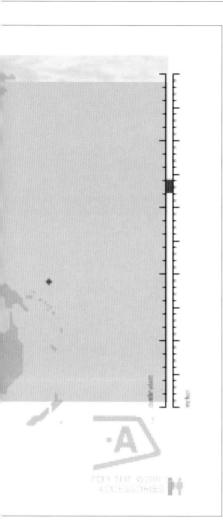

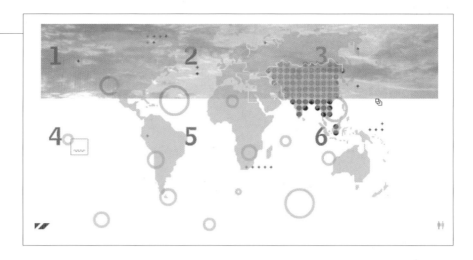

1 2 3

4 5 6

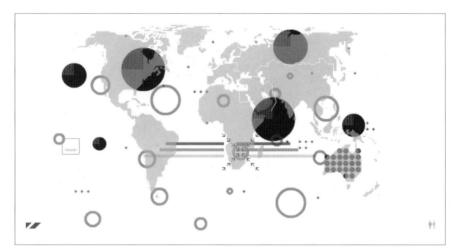

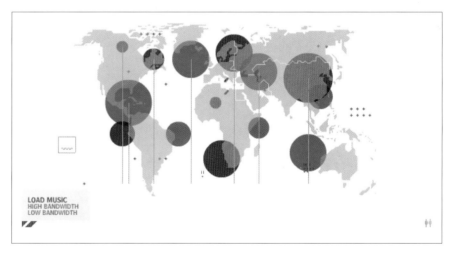

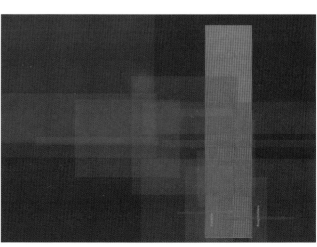

LOAD MUSIC
HIGH BANDWIDTH
LOW BANDWIDTH

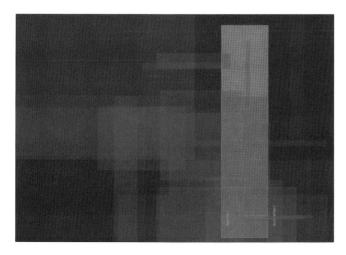

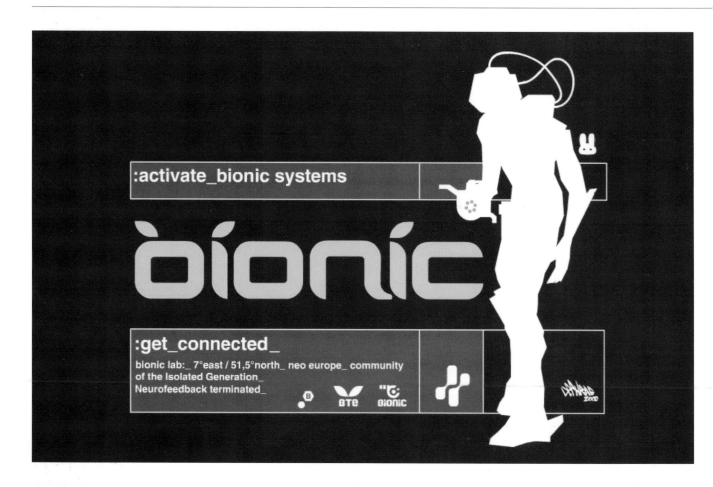

Düsseldorf, Germany
www.bionic-systems.com

Bionic Systems is the design firm of partners Doris Fürst and Malte Haust. The Bionic website presents their work in print media, poster design, and type design. The site incorporates robotic moving parts, and images of the designers themselves, connected to sensors and equipment; these are characteristic applications of their broader design sensibility, in which machine and man are often integrated. (In this, the web is an ideal vehicle for their particular design, as a medium that by definition unites people with their machines.) As they put it, "There's something strange and sexy about sharing our bodies with our technology. Whether it's with a computer, microwave oven, or minidisk player, there's an intimate relationship built between people and their technology. The further we evolve, the more enchanted we become with the idea of machine-assisted life." The site also showcases several typefaces the partners have created. The explosion of typeface design is part of a larger trend, says Haust: "Layout and other visual signifiers with a basis in web design will help standardize the visual language, per se. This will enable an immediate exchange of influences and ideas within a global context."

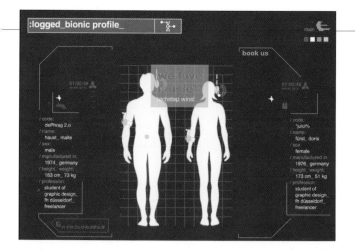

:logged_bionic profile_

book us

01:00:48

/ code:
dePhrag 2.0
/ name:
haust_ malte
/ sex:
male
/ manufactured in:
1974_ germany
/ height_ weight:
183 cm_ 73 kg
/ profession:
student of
graphic design_
fh düsseldorf_
freelancer

/ code:
"juici%
/ name:
fürst_ doris
/ sex:
female
/ manufactured in:
1976_ germany
/ height_ weight:
173 cm_ 51 kg
/ profession:
student of
graphic design_
fh düsseldorf_
freelancer

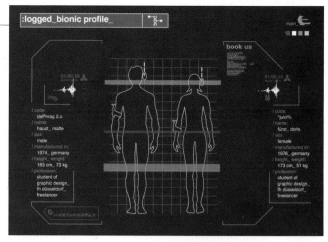

:logged_bionic profile_

main

book us

01:06:29

/ code:
dePhrag 2.0
/ name:
haust_ malte
/ sex:
male
/ manufactured in:
1974_ germany
/ height_ weight:
183 cm_ 73 kg
/ profession:
student of
graphic design_
fh düsseldorf_
freelancer

/ code:
"juici%
/ name:
fürst_ doris
/ sex:
female
/ manufactured in:
1976_ germany
/ height_ weight:
173 cm_ 51 kg
/ profession:
student of
graphic design_
fh düsseldorf_
freelancer

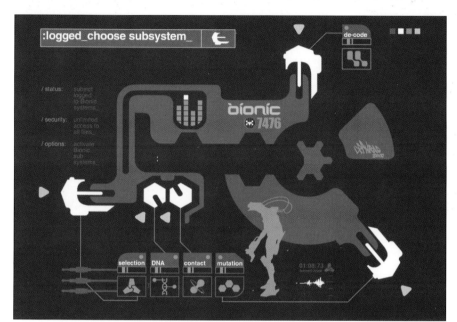

:logged_choose subsystem_

de-code

/ status: subject
logged
to Bionic
systems_

/ security: unlimited
access to
all files_

/ options: activate
Bionic
sub
systems_

bionic
7476

01:08:73

selection   DNA   contact   mutation

:bionic type engineering_fonts_

BTE basic
BTE bioterminal
BTE cyberwar
BTE discograf
BTE dorisOrange
BTE JuicyOrange
BTE orange out
BTE grand slam
BTE ten:fusion
BTE kitty
BTE seroppi
BTE sporty
BTE stereo bait 67

Doris
Orange

abcdefghijklmn
opqrstuuwxyz
ABCDEFGHIJKLMN
OPQRSTUUWXYZ
1234567890
Doris Orange

:logged_graphics: flyer

ultima ratio™
www.bionic-systems.com

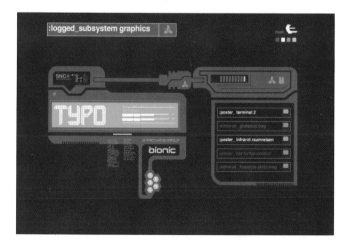

:logged_subsystem graphics

main

SNC

TYPO

bionic

:poster_ terminal 2

:editorial_ glutenal mag

:poster_ infrarot raumreisen

:poster_ bla fotopromotion

:editorial_ freestyle skillz mag

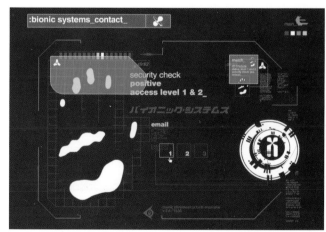

:bionic systems_contact_

main

security check
positive
access level 1 & 2_

email

1   2   3

Newport Beach, California
www.juxtinteractive.com

"It is a great time to be alive," writes Todd Purgason, creative director of Juxt Interactive. The design firm has an extensive client base, creating websites for several different industries. As their name implies, interactivity serves a prime function in their creative outlook. Juxt Interactive's commitment to communal principles extends to the open-sourcing of their codes. "We are often asked to share source codes, and we feel that it is good to offer up to the masses what we know, if it will help others out. It is about forming a dynamic relationship with the user, with design as one of the connection points. Interactivity is a relationship, and our work is meant to create personalities that users like to interrelate with." The structure of the site allows for further development and expansion, and the graphics themselves reflect this. "We design the site modularly and add new projects and news to it continuously. The home page is built to show the newest, most relevant stuff. The desktop section was built for our staff to add to as they will." Though the overall content of the site is continually evolving, the graphic setup is sectioned to allow for different types of design and graphic elements.

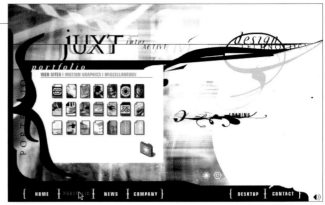

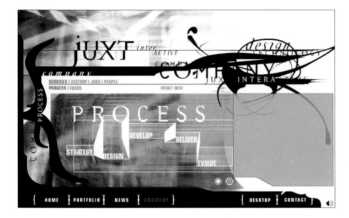

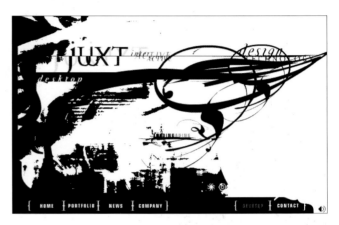

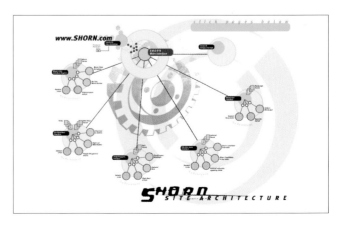

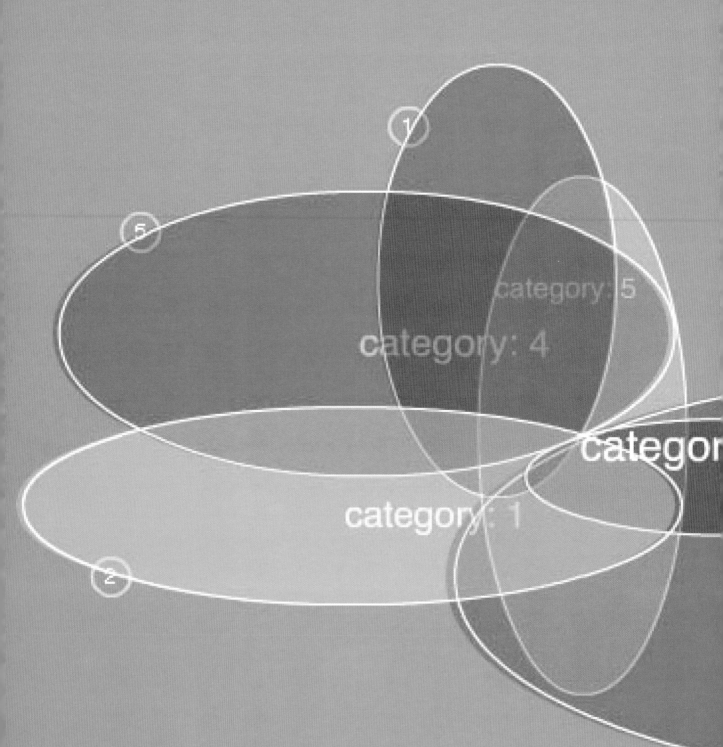

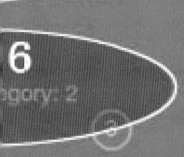

6

gory: 2

category: 3

SUTURE

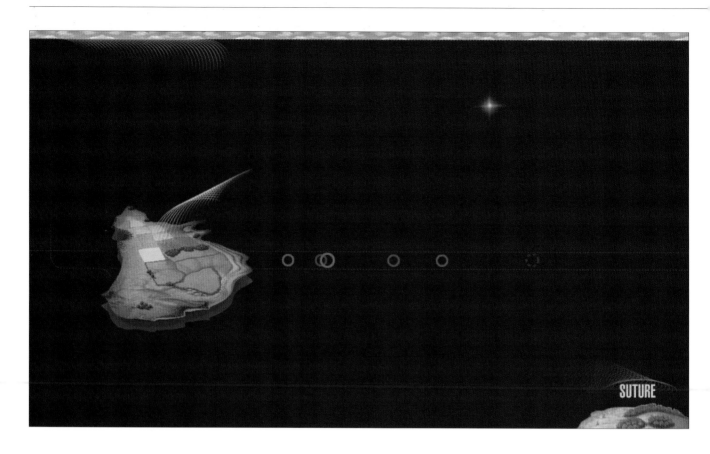

New York
www.suture.com

Jeremy Tai Abbett started Suture around the same time that he co-founded the design agency Fork Unstable Media in Hamburg a few years ago. "From the outset, I wanted to create a space where I could work out visual ideas as well as different forms of narrative expression." The site has developed into an autobiographical document that is continually evolving. The form of this work contrasts from print or analog media, in that it's possible for the user to experience the discovery of "artifacts"—in one instance, a series of letters linked to different parts of a map—which serve as clues to some larger history. The section on Vietnam is about self-discovery, considering his Vietnamese ancestry in light of the different phases of his life. Adopted into an American family as a child, Tai Abbett has an initial understanding of his origins that is naturally informed by the complicated relations between Vietnam and the U.S. After his move to Germany as an adult, Tai Abbett discovers an entirely different cultural perception of Vietnam. Finally, he visits his birthplace. As the name implies, Suture is about reuniting. This process is reflected in the site's structure: letters in pop-up windows linked to dates on a map supply fragments to the story, as do contemporary photographs shot by Tai Abbett from the back of a motorbike on the highway. The organization of material and the navigation through the site are overshadowed by the creator's moving personal account. In this regard, though site maps serve a valuable function, they seem to provide little more than an artificial structure. The evolution of the Suture site creates schisms in its own overall format, as Tai Abbett continues to search for meaning and connections among the events of his life.

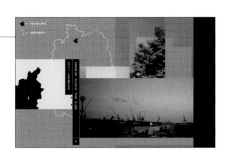

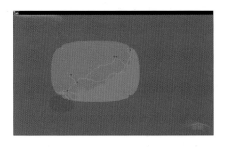

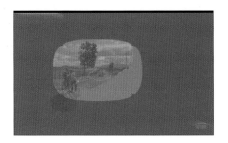

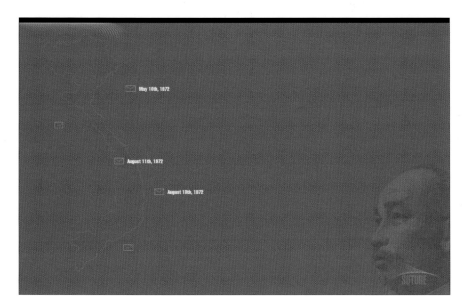

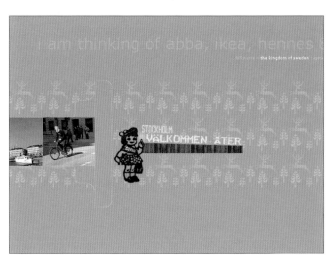

FUNKSTORUNG

enter fullscreen
enter 800.600

sounds and loops by
michael faiaach
text edit by
ps199 and andreas fischer
photos by
tina winkhaus and tobias ritz
scans by jeff ingram
sources by
praystation and flyoospace
powered by frank kirchner
basic design by
thedesignersrepublic
site design by leekon 10.2K

www.funkstorung.com

The website for the technomusic duo Funkstorung charts their tour dates, discography as well as broadcasting photographs and music samples. Organized into four sections, the contents on the site is graphically represented throughout by the site's interface, which makes up the top half of the site's screen. Rather than dividing its parts into different pages, the sections of the site are unified on one screen. Accessing each section prompts the various elements of the screen to slide about to make room for a sub-section to unfurl. The design and organizational concept for the site is to produce layout variations based on one simple theme. All the while the layout changes, the central block of the navigation—the graphic with four circular units—serves as a control panel to localize the user. The refined sensitivity to organization also extends to graphics and contents of the sections themselves. The use of different organizational methods is even a subtle and recurring theme in the site; examples of which range from the use a map and a question-and-answer section. The "links" section presents yet another graphic organization of contents. Two "three-dimensional" structures organize website links by genre, category, and name. The user can rotate either form, bringing a desired category of the links tree into closer proximity, or move it in its entirety. The interactive function of this element reflects the usage of graphic organization as a motif throughout the site. Similarly, it underscores how graphics themselves have become part and parcel of a site's contents.

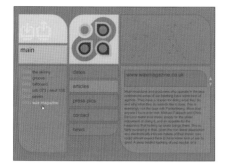

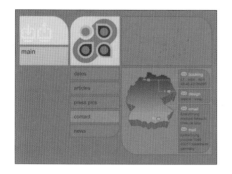

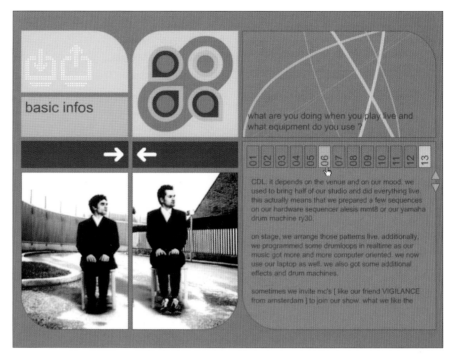

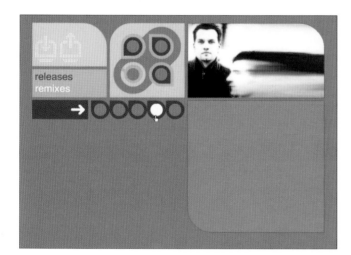

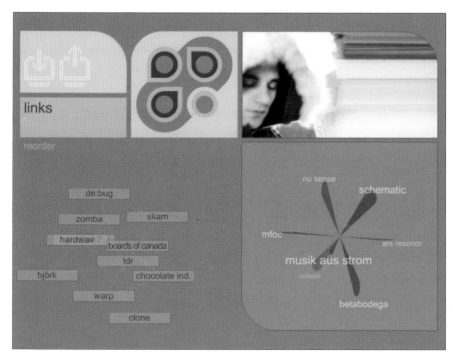

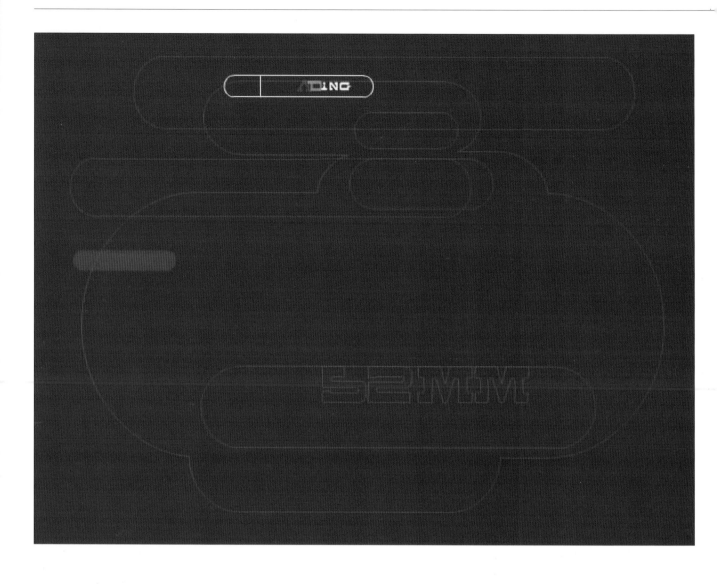

New York
www.52mm.com

The content of the 52mm site is organized into movable modules, rectangles that pop up on the all-red background. Rather than being presented in separate pages organized in a linear manner, all of the data and content are presented simultaneously on one page. Thus the process of finding connections within the various sections takes on a different form. The idea of linking and links becomes suspect, as the user makes visual and content-based connections in an apparently arbitrary manner. 52mm's creators, Marilyn Devedjiev and Katie Marsh, have divided the site's material into discrete modules, allowing for ease and flexibility in expanding or renewing information. They maintain that effective design can make use of interactive tools to stimulate the user's exploration of the site. This organizational structure has resulted in movable parts that allow the user to access different information and to create his own links within the material. This extended level of interaction renders the site itself an open-ended composition. Without the user—with his faculty to graphically, visually, or mentally organize the information available in the site—the site remains incomplete. To encourage and facilitate interaction, 52mm includes a series of movable tiles, which in turn provide texts or other downloads, such as graphics. Though not unique to 52mm, this expedient demonstrates a conceptual awareness of interactivity in the design.

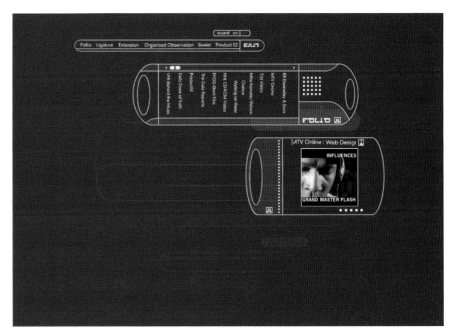

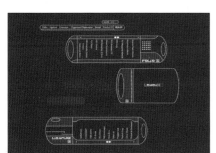

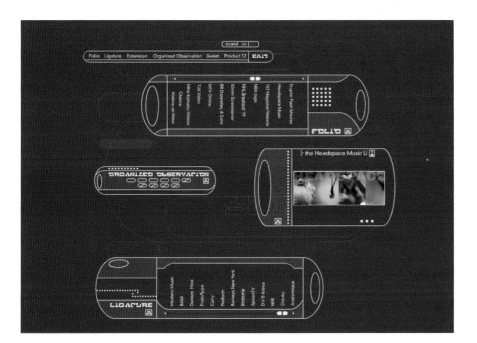

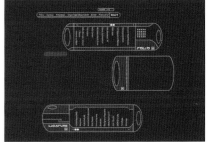

Flash navigation exploration design for 52mm client, ViOS.

London
www.wallpaper.com

The Wallpaper site was developed by I-D Media as a companion to the print life-style magazine *Wallpaper*. Taking its lead from the magazine's look, the website uses a combination of photography and illustration, collated with Flash. Like the magazine, the site deals with fashion and design editorial content, but also includes an on-line dinner-party seating-arrangement consultation, advice on wine, an archive of travel tips for various global destinations, and more. As an example of the possible implementations of e-commerce, the site has essentially translated the style of the magazine onto the web. In this regard, the website is but one arm of a large media campaign. However, the site does provide a number of auxiliary components to the experience of the magazine, such as sound, interactivity, and gratis items and services: a Wallpaper e-mail address, screen savers, and greeting cards. Eventually, the site will have an e-commerce function as an on-line shopper's haven for products that are also featured in the print magazine. While many companies affect an affiliation with the web by intentionally using pixilated or "rough" graphics, Wallpaper has steered clear of this. In fact, the site seems devoid of web graphics per se, and relies heavily on the image and style of the magazine. *Wallpaper* magazine has thus been able to propagate its specific brand image through the use of its website, demonstrating that slick web graphics are not mandatory for an effective on-line presence.

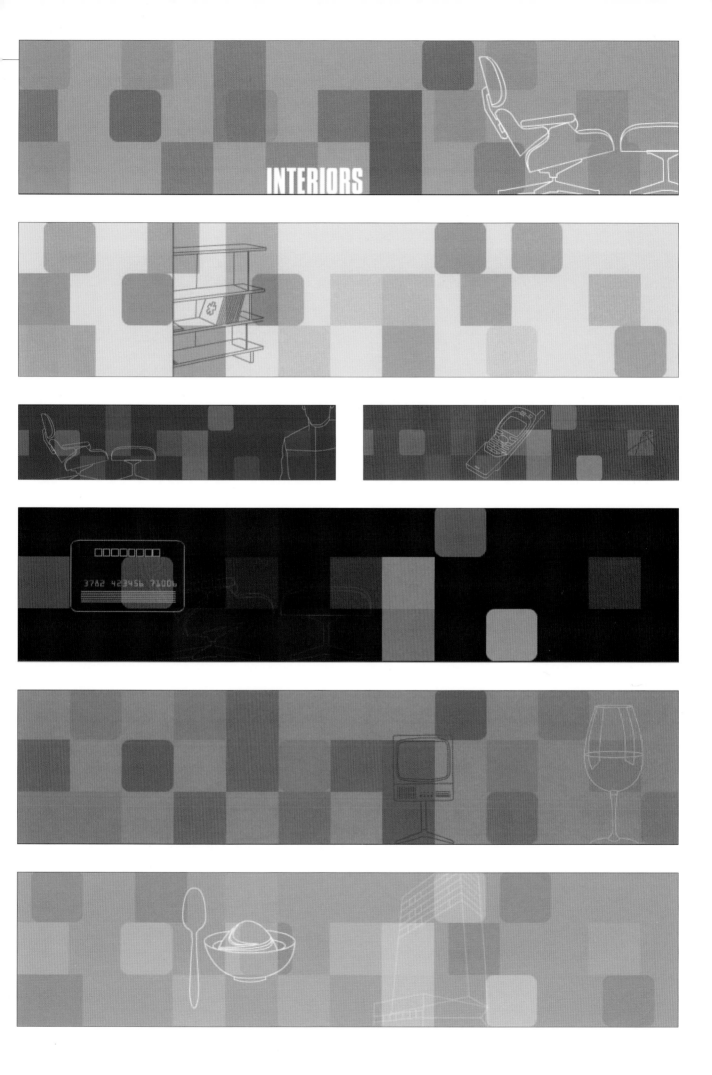

INTERIORS

003

GROUPDYNAMICS
Put your guests in order – ensure they're strategically placed around the dinner table

ENTERTAINING

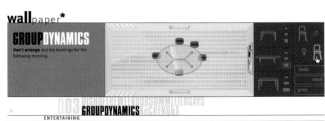

GROUPDYNAMICS
Don't arrange any big meetings for the following morning.

ENTERTAINING

Sancerre Rose

Dezat, 1999

Pinot Noir is the grape behind this rose gorgeous tint. At the top of its class, this fresh, dry wine is from one of the best areas on the planet for blush wines. (It certainly brought colour to our cheeks.) Black cherry and forest raspberry give it its depth of flavour, it full-bodied and is at its drinking peak just in time for summer. If only days were longer and the bottle was bigger.

01 02 03 PINK FLUSH

OURSOMMELIERSAYS

ENTERTAINING

WALLPAPER*PUMATRAINERS
Retail Price: go.coUKP (including postage and packaging)
Delivery: Within 10 days
Customer Service Tel: +44 (0) 207 322 1382, Fax: +44 (0) 207 322 1171
Customer Service e-mail: sales@wallpaper.com
Payment: Credit card (Visa, MasterCard, AMEX, Access)
Cheque: Made payable to Wallpaper*. Send to: Brettenham House, Lancaster Place, London, WC2E 7TL, United Kingdom.
(must have credit card number/cheque guarantee number on back and expiry date)

TRAINERS

W*WARE

Wallpaper* has positioned itself from its inception as an international magazine for international consumers. Its readers live in London, Tokyo, Stockholm, Paris, Sydney, Hamburg, Hong Kong and New York. Wallpaper's research into its UK subscribers has found that in London they live in prosperous enclaves, affluent city areas or gentrified multi-ethnic areas. They have been described as predominantly single or unmarried couples, highly qualified executives and young professionals (Acorn).

THEREADER

W*?

ourglobalforum
Dialogue on design and the events of the day.

GLOBALFORUM

CONSULAR SERVICES

1YEAR SUBSCRIPTION
10issues

2YEAR SUBSCRIPTION
20issues

W*SUBSCRIPTION

W*?

NEWYORKICFF

INTELLIGENCE

wallpaper*

THE NAVIGATOR
Argentine Rose: Making the most of South America's chicest city

1:100

NAVIGATOR
TRAVEL

UPGRADES
DOWNGRADES
Our global travel advisory

UPGRADES&DOWNGRADES
TRAVEL

wallpaper*

buenos aires **navigator**

places to stay
places to eat/drink
places to shop
places to see
ten things you must buy
ten things you must do
websites
useful numbers

Avenida Cordoba
Viamonte
le los pozos
LAvenidaalle
Corrientes
Sarimento
Cangallo
Sarimento

From dusk to dawn: the best places to go exploring, party the night away, then rest your weary bones

+ 1:1 −

NAVIGATOR

TRAVEL

wallpaper*

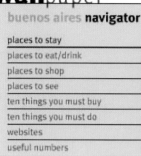

CASABLANCA   1/22

Very much a 20th-century creation, Casablanca owes its existence to the French, who decided, back in 1907, to construct a major port on what was then a stretch of barren Atlantic coast. In 1915, after annexing the rest of Morocco, they laid out a city for 150,000 people with the aid of aerial photography. Everyone said they were mad, but the new city

HUBBING
TRAVEL

wallpaper*

THE FUTURE   4/22

Casablanca remains Morocco's business hub, with its own stock market, and as such is not particularly geared up for tourism. But there are signs of change, as the city begins to wake up to its rich legacy of 20th-century architecture. Casablanca's first museum is on the cards, and a consortium of tour operators is planning a marina to attract the cruise-liner crowd. So if you have a day in Morocco to spare, spare it for Casablanca. You might not meet Ingrid Bergman, but you will see Africa's best Art Deco, and the tallest minaret on earth.

HUBBING
TRAVEL

wallpaper*

JUNE 2000
- The horrendous duty free that attacks you when walking out of customs at Heathrow's terminal one
- The rash of corporate high-rises taking over Shanghai
- The cabana rooms at the Hilton in Athens - way too small
- The tacky kiosks that have started to clutter Hong Kong airport
- Horrendous roadworks and start of the tourist season in London double trouble

DOWNGRADE UPGRAD

UPGRADES&DOWNGRADES
TRAVEL

wallpaper*

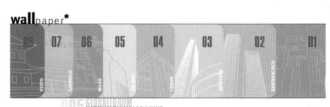

08 07 06 05 04 03 02 01

KYOTO SAO PAULO MILAN LISBON AUCKLAND SAN FRANCISCO

INTERNATIONALARCHIVE
CONSULAR SERVICES

wallpaper*

kyoto **navigator**
places to stay
places to eat/drink
places to shop
architecture
ten things you must buy
ten things you must do
who, what, where & when
useful numbers

Marutamachidori St.
NAKAGYO-KU
Nijojo Castle
Oikerdori St.
Shindori St.

tatami, temples, tea ceremonies - take in Japan at its most trad*

+ 1:1 −

wallpaper*

FABULOUS FABLE

FABULOUSFABLE
TRAVEL

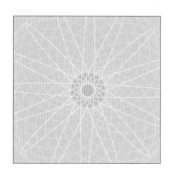

Welcome to the Chill Room

FIVE MINUTES LATER:

One of Becky's young millionaire friends accused me of drinking all of his orange juice. Actually, what he said was, "Becky, that Marlboro Man uncle of yours hogged all my Gatorade." I corrected him and told him that this "Gator" drink was not orange juice at all, and was, in fact, free of citrus altogether.

In turn, he said I was, "the only human being he'd ever met with wood paneling." Was this a put down? Was it a put up? I think it was his way of saying to me, "Philip, you're a good egg after all." Young people truly embrace me. It is my gift.

7/8

Bristol
www.ward7.co.uk

With its building-block colors and the assembly of levers and knobs in the initial interface, the Ward 7 site resembles a game for building a virtual model-railway system—with the user playing the part of the conductor. The different-colored modules move along tracks, controlled either by the user's mouse or by his keyboard; this simultaneously reveals and conceals the site's menus, as they slide in and out of view. Flash is used to animate blocks and graphics, following a setup that resembles miniature train or racing-car sets. Indeed, the entire site is unified around the navigational principle of racing-car sets, as seen in its spin on product branding, which can be manipulated much like a model construction site. The user can choose between two un-labeled products and create his own mock-brand image. This relatively benign fun soon takes on a rather cynical feel, and the very content of the site—a veritable Candyland of miniature ships, tiny plastic trees, and Erector Set braces—becomes a send-up of the ubiquitous "cute and clever" aesthetics that characterize much current web design. (At the same time, it is not entirely clear whether or not this cynicism extends to the artificial environment of the Ward 7 site itself.) The programming here is sophisticated and the graphic elements are polished; the creators' goal is to create a "three-dimensional" representation of movement, visually organized by a set of miniature pieces (again, much like the parts of a model train or racing-car set).

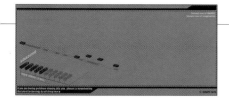

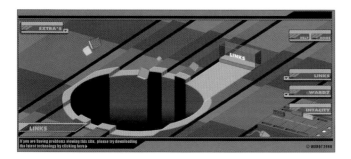

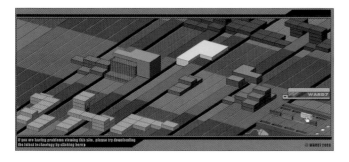

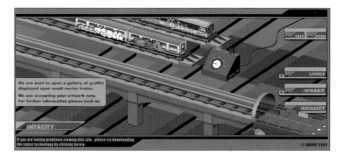

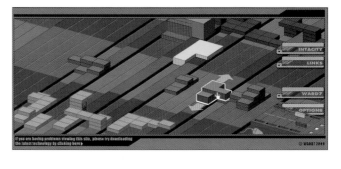

New York
www.pre-loaded.com

One effective expedient in the organization and simplification of websites is a single graphic element that can serve both to unify the site and also as the prime navigational tool for the user. The web-content and design firm Preloaded created a site by the same name to showcase their work and provide a portal, with restricted access, for their clients. As the site's creators explain: "We wanted to create an interface that would facilitate exploration on a number of levels, allowing the user to get as much, or as little, information as desired. The tuning and channel metaphor allows us to add or remove any content we wish, whenever we want, without it being a complicated process. Plus, the retro feel of the TV and games makes a nice juxtaposition with the technology we specialize in, at a time when convergence is obviously an issue for us and other companies in our field." As consultants and creators in the realm of the new media field, they needed to have a strong presence on the web. "It was important for us to build a site, which showed what Preloaded was about, and what kind of work we were interested in creating. Our site says more about us as an agency than any traditional sales pitch or brochure-ware offering could. We wanted something that was more of an experience, one that would draw people in to wanting to ask more about us directly. We hope it will attract the kind of people we want to have conversations with. . . ." While the use of the TV set as a navigational tool gives the creators versatility with the site's content, the decidedly retro look is a salient graphic metaphor that provides a recognizable icon for the ever-shrinking non-virtual world. Compared to their competitors' sophisticated visual spaces, the sparse look of Preloaded seems effortless and grounded in reality.

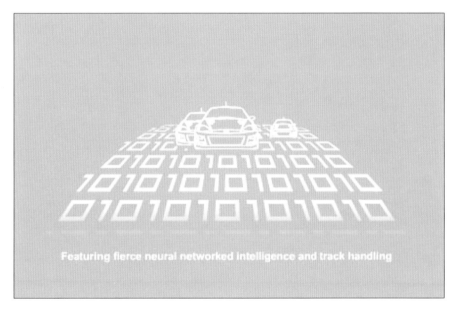

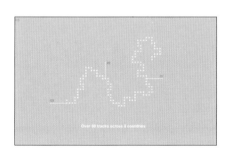

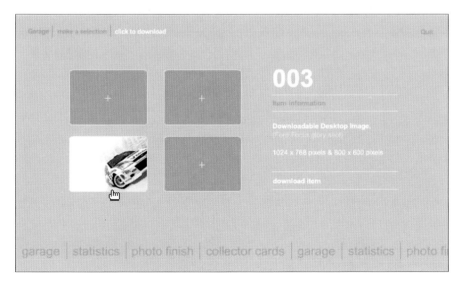

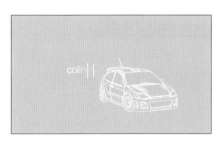

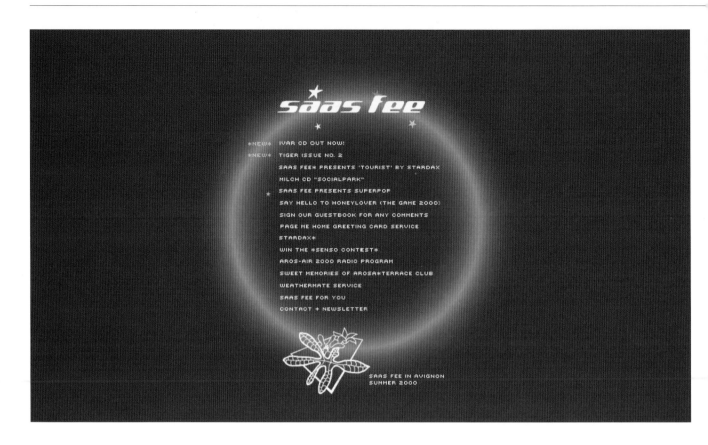

Offenbach, Germany
www.saasfee.de

The Saas Fee site was originally called Arosa 2000 after a Frankfurt shop-cum-exhibition venue that began in 1994. Profoundly interested in developing new forms of presentation, and in connecting an innovative and powerful pool of creative people with new domains, the site's founders (Alex Oppermann, Moni Friebe, Axel Rossler, Al Dhanab, Malte Tinnus, and Valentin Beinroth) staged various events in the Arosa 2000 gallery space: exhibitions, workshops, presentations of movies, musical events, and installations. A network of collaborators formed as the projects grew in number and variety. One of these projects was the creation of the Saas Fee website, which now features an expanding program of activities, including music releases and CD-ROMs (with short films, videos, and animations). The Saas Fee site is the result of collaborative efforts of artists, designers, music-ians, and programmers. The graphic elements and design of the site reflect this collaborative approach, with different pages of the site visually organized according to the project. Elements range from a video game with movable parts to a digital art book that the user can flip through, to a page of sounds that "ignite" in response to the user's cursor. Dismissing the restrictions of visual cohesion and unity, the site presents an array of graphics that plainly evolve from the projects. As such, the development of the Saas Fee site is not self-contained. It is part of a larger roster of activities and the contents, graphics, and design of the website reflect this, providing a range of web experiences that help expand the dimension of content on the web.

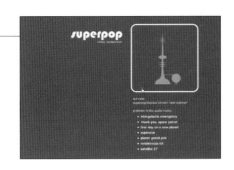

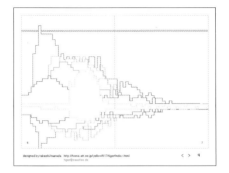

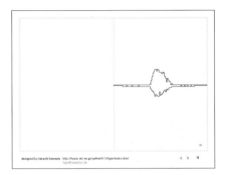

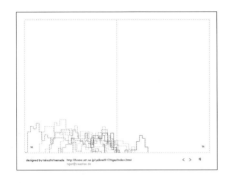

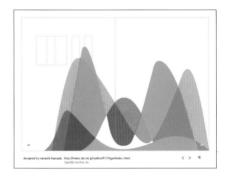

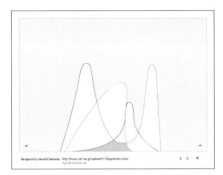

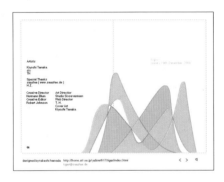

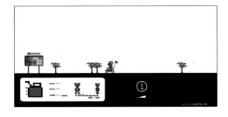

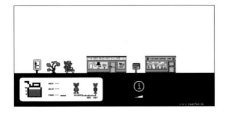

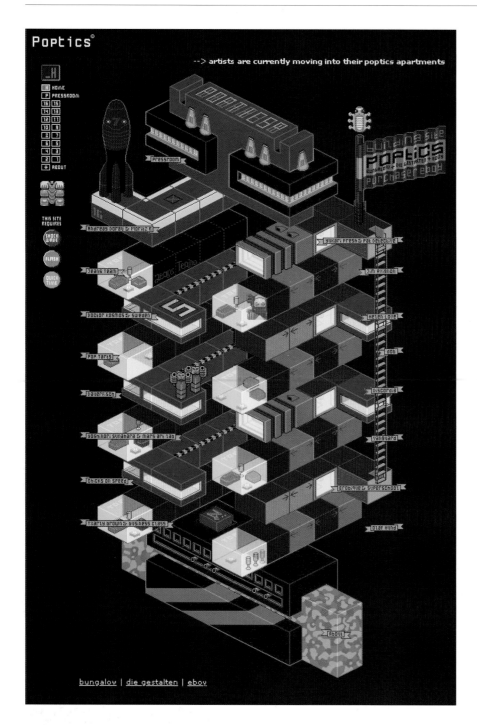

Berlin & New York
www.poptics.com

Poptics was created to provide a democratic representation for a spectrum of artists, achieved through the graphic elements for interactive navigation. The initial concept was that the site would function as a digital artists-in-residence setup, giving each artist their own virtual "bungalow" and stacking all the bungalows on top of one another. The small-sized numbers at the side represents floor numbers inside an elevator. The main site interface was designed and programmed by Eboy. The original idea for the Poptics site was conceived by Bungalow Records, as a new way to reach people and to publish the last pop songs of the end of the last millennium.

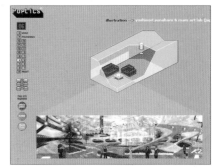

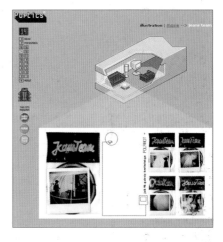

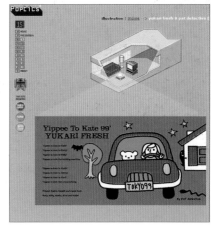

New York
www.bowienet.com

Working with a well-established artist like David Bowie seems like it might present something of a challenge for designers trying to create a website that stands on its own merits. But for the creators of the Bowienet site, art director/lead designer De Angela Duff and her team, the problem was negligible. "The initial development of the site's visual concept began with a meeting with David Bowie himself. With Bowienet version 1.0, our theme was chaos and disorder. With Bowienet version 2.0, architecture, space, and viruses were the themes that Bowie wanted to pursue. When you are given complete creative freedom, design is exploration; risks are taken; and innovation motivates the process. However, if the design is initially imposed with constraints and a cookie-cutter mentality, the design solutions [will be] confined and not as creative, let alone innovative. Working with Bowie . . . is a designer's dream. Once he communicated the visual concepts he wanted us to explore, he allowed us to do what we do best: design. He respected us as designers and did not look over our shoulders or question any of our design, interactivity, and user interface decisions." The central goal of Bowienet is for the user to experience total immersion in the site. The opening trailer is a montage of Bowie's images through the years, and the words "Make me and re-make me." Further in, Bowienet continues the line of re-creation, even allowing the user to re-mix Bowie's music on-line. Toward this goal of immersion, the site uses the latest technologies for interaction.

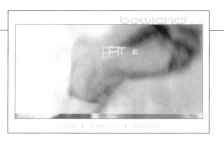

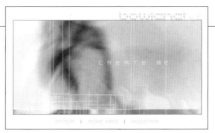

ENTER | MORE INFO | REGISTER

ENTER | MORE INFO | REGISTER

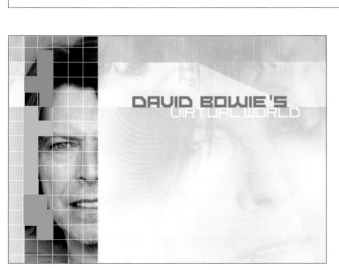

DAVID BOWIE'S
VIRTUAL WORLD

.01
LO
MED
HI

.02
LO
MED
HI

LO
.03 MED
HI

SELECT A SEGMENT

DAVID BOWIE'S
VIRTUAL WORLD

Watch the recording of the cybersong contest winning
entry, "What's Really Happening", take a tour of BowieNet,
and take a peek at virtual Bowie in Omikron: The Nomad
soul. The "perennial polymedia man" discusses the
internet, BowieNet, his experience online, and his
opinion on MP3s and the future of the web.

Paris
www.kOzen.com
www.kenzo.com

As a part of fashion-designer Kenzo's eponymous website, the Kozen (pronounced *kao-zen*) site is presented in the style of a magazine. With its focus on culture and articles on art, design, and fashion, Kozen is reaching out to a wide community of users. The site is designed by the Parisian agencies The_link and Subakt, under the artistic direction of Philippe Moyen; and the magazine's content is generated in London, Stockholm, Italy, Spain, and Tokyo. As the site's creator Mathias Ohrel describes it, Kozen was created in order to "give Kenzo a strong web identity, conveying and bringing to life the Kenzo spirit, while enriching Kenzo's current brand values. . . . The goal is to create new inspiration: innovative, cultural, and creative inspiration around the Kenzo brand. This is the direct translation of the metamorphosis currently underway at Kenzo and the new impetus desired for the brand." As he explains, Kenzo's website concept is based on the union of two different worlds: Chaos and Zen. This is an attitude, a life-style, and an outlook on current cultural and creative events, that reaches beyond the realm of fashion.

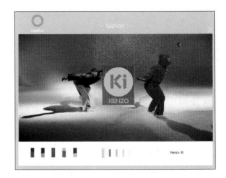
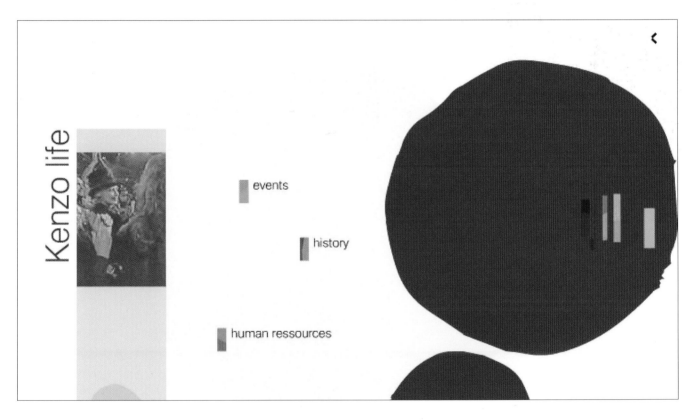
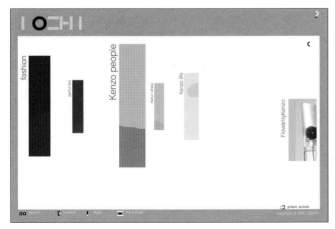
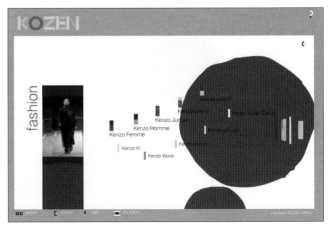

New York
www.hintmag.com

Fashion is a giant commercial realm that, like everything else, is looking for an identity on the web. Riding on the coattails of larger advertising campaigns and print-media fashion magazines, web-based fashion publications are still in their relative infancy. Interactivity, in an industry notorious for being inaccessible, comes as something of a shock. Still, it provides a valuable tool for retailers to gather market information and to build a secondary clientele base across several segments of the consumer market. But even well-established brands are no match for the slew of new sites that utilize clever and innovative design. Most design houses simply opt to translate their brand image onto a website; function, apart from marketing, is almost nonexistent. On the other hand, independent on-line fashion magazines do offer a lot of channels for following the fashion industry, catering to a younger audience. Hint Magazine is one of the more innovative of these on-line publications. Intended to resemble a print fashion magazine, complete with features and original photography, the site is enhanced with the dimensions of interactivity, sound, and animation. Interactivity plays a key role in users' experience on Hint, but—as in print media—the basic composition of a page is still the most important priority. When choosing photography for the site, its creator Lee Carter looks for "clean shapes, bold colors, and perfect skin tone." An appreciation for the subdued and simple marks a sharp contrast to the "chaos" that is generated on the web by "overzealous designers," quips Carter.

the outsider

photos Ronald Stoops
styling Stephen Jones
makeup Inge Grognard

1 2 3 4

1 2 3

1 2 4

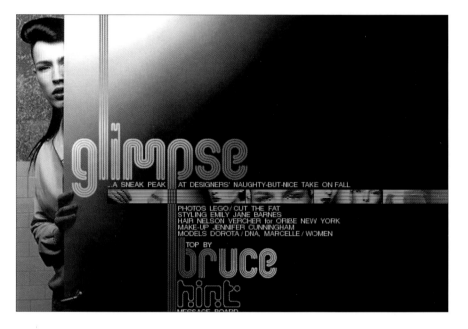

glimpse

...A SNEAK PEAK AT DESIGNERS' NAUGHTY-BUT-NICE TAKE ON FALL

PHOTOS LEGO/ CUT THE FAT
STYLING EMILY JANE BARNES
HAIR NELSON VERCHER for ORIBE NEW YORK
MAKE-UP JENNIFER CUNNINGHAM
MODELS DOROTA / DNA, MARCELLE / WOMEN

TOP BY

bruce

h.int
MESSAGE BOARD

clarina bezzola
for bruce

VEIL VINTAGE
GOLD NET TOP BY

h.int
MESSAGE BOARD

miguel adrover
TOP AND SKIRT BY

h.int
MESSAGE BOARD

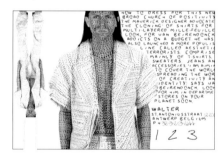

WALTER
ST.ANTONIUSSTRAAT
ANTWERP BELGIUM

1 2 3

BY GLENN BELVERIO
PHOTOS BY RONALD STOOPS

HAVING SEVERED TIES WITH HIS FORMER BACKERS—AN ACRIMONIOUS SPLIT IN WHICH HE LOST NAMING RIGHTS TO WILD & LETHAL TRASH (W.&.L.T.), THE FUNKY LINE FAVORED BY JAPANESE RAVERS AND U2—WALTER VAN BEIRENDONCK IS BACK DESIGNING UNDER HIS OWN NAME. AND, JUDGING BY THE STARSHIP EARTH COLLECTION HE SHOWED DURING NEW YORK FASHION WEEK, THE DESIGNER WHO LIT A ROCKET UNDER THE ASS OF RETRO FASHION IS STILL SPACEY AFTER ALL THESE YEARS.

PLANETWALT

2 3 4

VAN BEIRENDONCK HAS ALWAYS EXISTED ON A PARALLEL FASHION PLANET-EVER MODERN AND SLIGHTLY OUT THERE, TRUE TO FORM, THE STARSHIP EARTH COLLECTION FOR SPRING 200X IS AN HOMAGE TO THE FUTURIST WRITING OF BUCKMINSTER FULLER, THE ARCHITECT/PROPHET WHO COINED THE TERM "IT TELLS SO MUCH ABOUT OUR RELATION WITH THE EARTH AND OUR TRAVEL-OUR LIFE ON PLANET EARTH" EXPLAINS THE DESIGNER

1 3 4

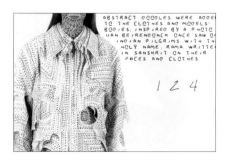

ABSTRACT DOODLES WERE ADDED TO THE CLOTHES AND MODELS' BODIES, INSPIRED BY A PHOTO VAN BEIRENDONCK ONCE SAW OF INDIAN PILGRIMS WITH THE HOLY NAME, RAMA, WRITTEN IN SANSKRIT ON THEIR FACES AND CLOTHES.

1 2 4

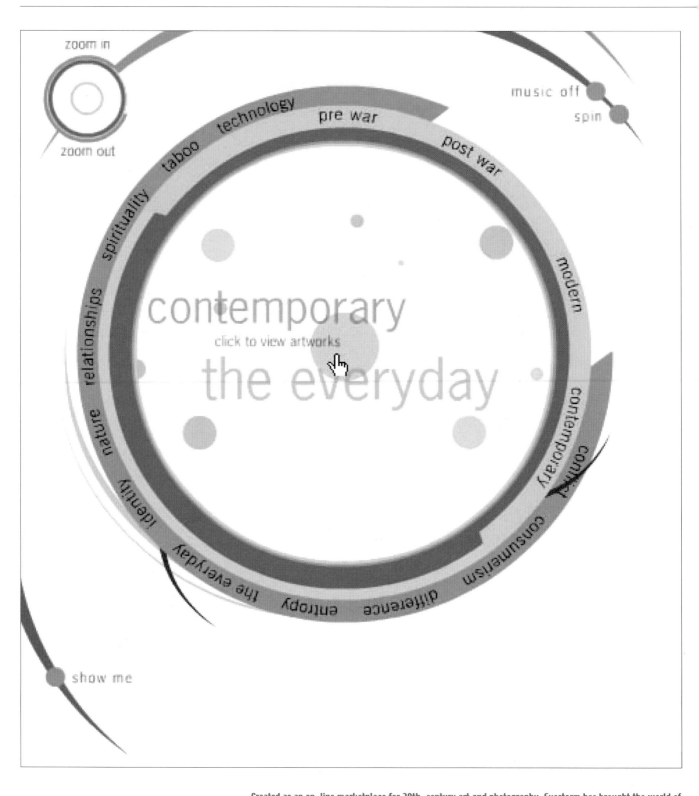

New York
www.eyestorm.com

Created as an on-line marketplace for 20th-century art and photography, Eyestorm has brought the world of art-buying into the laissez-faire realm of internet sales. The spectrum of artists represented on the site is broad, including such popular names as Jeff Koons and Andy Warhol. Though it does not yet pose a threat to the gallery system of art sales, Eyestorm does offer a potential new route for art-collecting. The work that is available for purchase on the site is organized in a rotating set of concentric graphics, resembling a camera's aperture: the user may specify what genre, artist, period, theme, or content he's interested in. Organizing art in such categories can present limitations to a work's interpretation and meaning. Therefore, the rotating rings of the central graphic on the site, paired with a "three-dimensional" site map in the center of the main graphic, show all the categories simultaneously. This enables cross-referencing and various groupings of different art, thereby avoiding the claptrap of categorization.

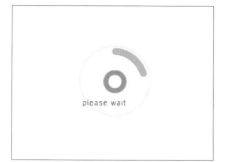

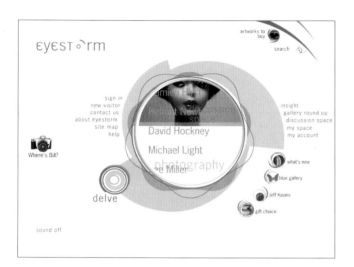

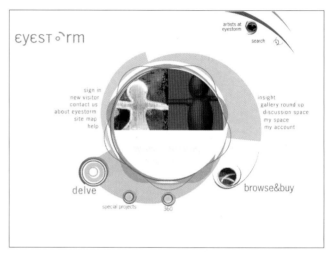

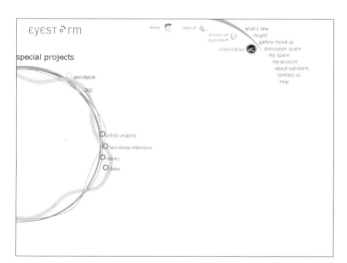

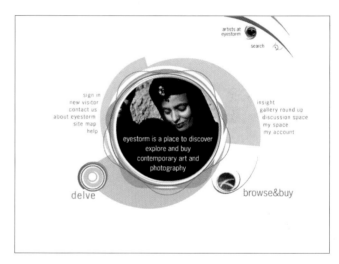

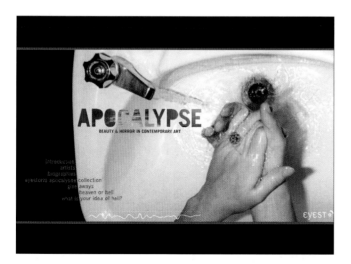

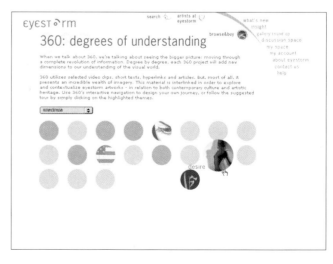

DENNIS INTERACTIVE

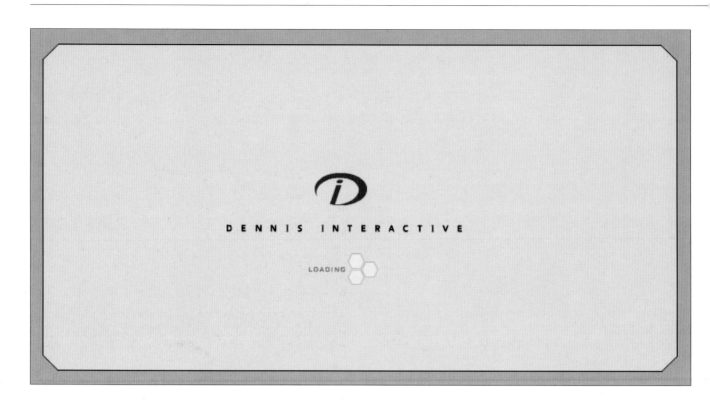

New York
www.dennisinter.com

Web-design firm Dennis Interactive, well-known to the industry for its innovative ideas, has created sites and kiosks for a range of clients, from car manufacturers to architectural firms. Representing their own distinctive skills, the Dennis website was created to reflect the growth of the design team and the company as a whole. Begun by Dennis Interactive's creative director Justin Crawford, the original site's signature navigation hexagons and button icons have persisted through its evolution, right up to the present version of the site. Such core visual elements—fundamental to the design concept of the site—have not changed over time, even though the graphics are now animated (and sometimes even explosive). If anything, the technological innovations available to the designers have only served to establish the original design of the site more firmly. For the creators of Dennis, it is of paramount importance that the site should remain in the user's memory for a prolonged time, and that a strong and unified brand identity is recognizable on the web. This latter imperative—important to any commercial design endeavor—is crucial in web design.

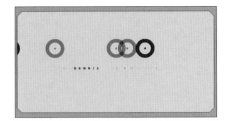

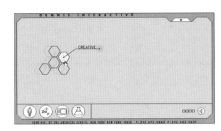
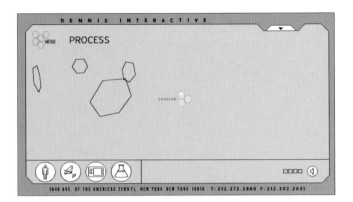
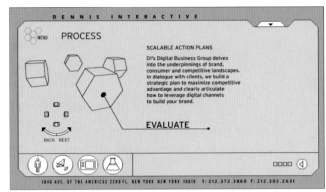
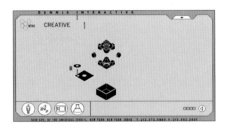

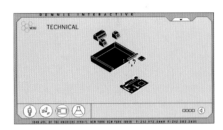
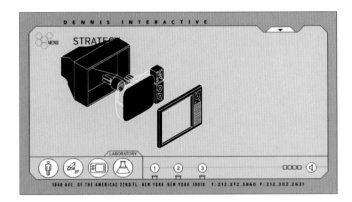
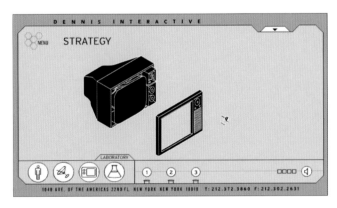
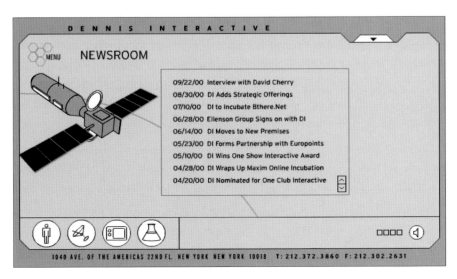

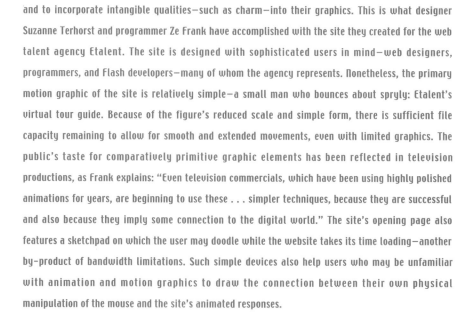

New York
www.etalentagency.com

To date, motion graphics have generally been used in web design with a fair amount of abandon and little regard for necessity. However, technical restrictions compel web designers to be resourceful and to incorporate intangible qualities—such as charm—into their graphics. This is what designer Suzanne Terhorst and programmer Ze Frank have accomplished with the site they created for the web talent agency Etalent. The site is designed with sophisticated users in mind—web designers, programmers, and Flash developers—many of whom the agency represents. Nonetheless, the primary motion graphic of the site is relatively simple—a small man who bounces about spryly: Etalent's virtual tour guide. Because of the figure's reduced scale and simple form, there is sufficient file capacity remaining to allow for smooth and extended movements, even with limited graphics. The public's taste for comparatively primitive graphic elements has been reflected in television productions, as Frank explains: "Even television commercials, which have been using highly polished animations for years, are beginning to use these . . . simpler techniques, because they are successful and also because they imply some connection to the digital world." The site's opening page also features a sketchpad on which the user may doodle while the website takes its time loading—another by-product of bandwidth limitations. Such simple devices also help users who may be unfamiliar with animation and motion graphics to draw the connection between their own physical manipulation of the mouse and the site's animated responses.

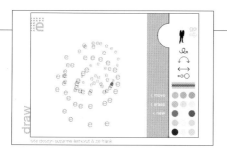

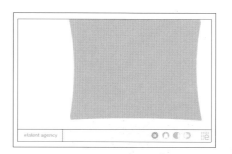

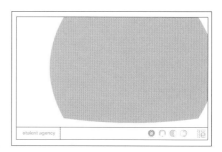

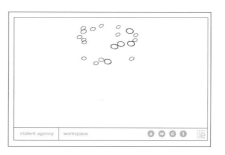

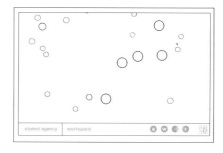

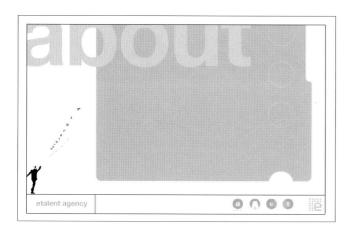

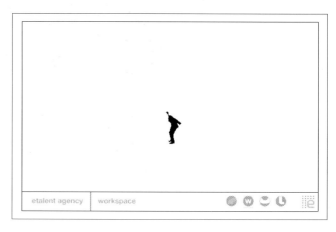

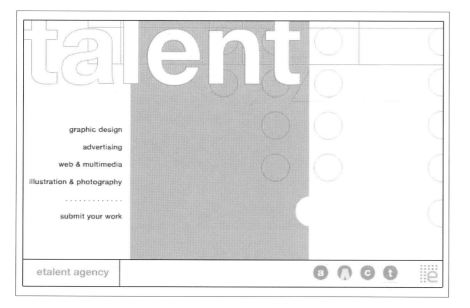

London
www.johnjohnrecords.com

The John John Records website is a promotional tool for the musicians signed to the John John label. The founders of the music label are themselves designers and creators (web-designer and musician Benoit Viellefon, illustrator and graphic-designer Christine Boulanger, and music producer Peter Dry). (The sister site, www.johnjohn.co.uk, demonstrates these other faculties.) Started with the commercial directive to broadcast good music by good musicians, John John Records was an solution for musicians frustrated with the music industry. The site is geared toward gaining exposure for the bands they represent. Viellefon writes, "We've chosen to use the internet because it is possible to compete with very large companies even if you are really small. It is the quality of the design, interface, and content that brings people back to a site—not the amount of money spent on the marketing campaign. As we love music, fine arts, animation, and comics, we thought that many people would have the same frustration in front of the austerity of the net. This is why we've designed this site that way. We deliberately opted for an illustrative style with characters. We wanted the site to be pleasant and refreshing so that people would come back and show it to their friends. We try to give the maximum exposure to the bands and artists with pictures, interviews, and lots of other things. We put up some games and invite people to copy them on their sites, and there are lots of community features available." Boulanger continues, "At the time when Benoit had the idea to create two characters in a cartoon style, web design was full of cyber-brand-new-modern stuff, very serious, futuristic, and often cold and meaningless. We decided that we didn't need to look serious and uptight to look professional. One thing that's a bit odd about being a web designer is spending all day in front of a computer screen, so the last thing I want to see when I go on the internet is something boring that reminds me that I am actually watching a vulgar screen! Not long ago, there was still a big trend for a kind of science-fiction design because of the fascination for this new media, . . . and all the futuristic fantasies around it. This style could be beautifully used sometimes but was often cold and lacking a bit of humor, of human touch. Now the style seems to be more various, with perhaps a preponderance of cartoons. Web designers should be especially careful with trends and avoid them. The design has to match the content, not the fashion. Information moves very fast on the web; fashion gets old fast too." Viellefon and Boulanger continue to look for new clients to represent and also plan to add a gallery for fine artists and comic books.

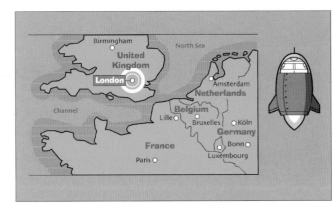

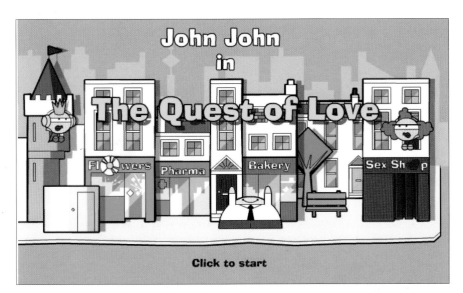

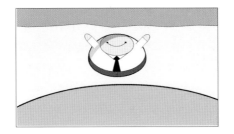

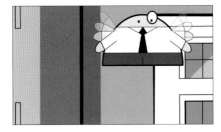

AERIFORM

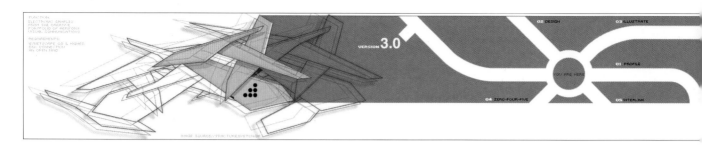

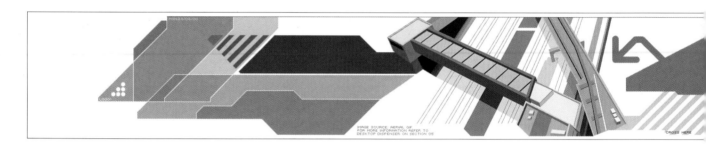

London
www.aeriform.co.uk

The design duo of Sean Rodwell and Angela Carter created their website Aeriform in the remarkably brief period of two weeks. The look and feel of the site came about after they'd decided to pull the plug on Version 2, the site's previous incarnation. Rodwell and Carter were still inexperienced at building sites, and their ideas were not working as planned. They decided that a new site had to be built from scratch. "It still baffles me how the visual aspect came about," says Rodwell. "I was playing around in Photoshop, and a style started emerging, sort of a really clean, crisp, technical look but with a kind of free-style, almost graffiti feel to it. This was then set next to minimal gray spaces with clean typography, and the Aeriform look was there." Used as a commercial tool to generate more design work for the duo, the website was successful in attracting a lot of attention. Aeriform was linked to K10K, and soon thereafter began receiving unexpectedly high numbers of hits per day. As Rodwell says: "With the web, to me, it's all about immediate impact. You need to captivate the viewer as soon as the first page loads or else you'll lose them. We're all guilty of this: if something doesn't grab your attention upon load up, you leave. Also, I have a bit of a problem with huge Flash files for splash pages. Flash is seriously misused at the moment, with people feeling they need to create 500k files that, in the end, serve no real purpose. Having said all this, the net still remains the most inspiring place to conduct your activities."

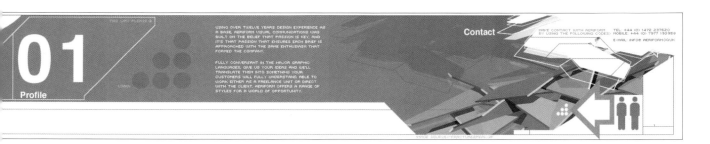

01
Profile

USING OVER TWELVE YEARS DESIGN EXPERIENCE AS A BASE, AERIFORM VISUAL COMMUNICATIONS WAS BUILT ON THE BELIEF THAT PASSION IS KEY, AND IT'S THAT PASSION THAT ENSURES EACH BRIEF IS APPROACHED WITH THE SAME ENTHUSIASM THAT FORMED THE COMPANY.

FULLY CONVERSANT IN THE MAJOR GRAPHIC LANGUAGES, GIVE US YOUR IDEAS AND WE'LL TRANSLATE THEM INTO SOMETHING YOUR CUSTOMERS WILL FULLY UNDERSTAND. ABLE TO WORK EITHER AS A FREELANCE UNIT OR DIRECT WITH THE CLIENT, AERIFORM OFFERS A RANGE OF STYLES FOR A WORLD OF OPPORTUNITY.

Contact

MAKE CONTACT WITH AERIFORM   TEL. +44 (0) 1472 237620
BY USING THE FOLLOWING CODES: MOBILE: +44 (0) 7977 195959
E-MAIL: INFO@ AERIFORM.CO.UK

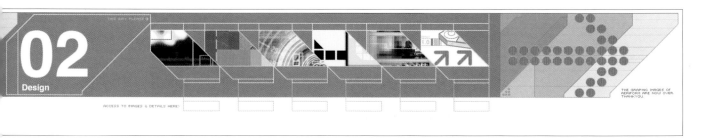

02
Design

ACCESS TO IMAGES & DETAILS HERE:

THE GRAPHIC IMAGES OF AERIFORM ARE NOW OVER. THANKYOU.

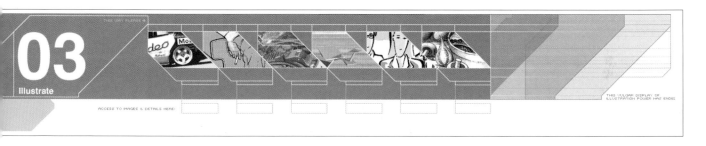

03
Illustrate

ACCESS TO IMAGES & DETAILS HERE:

THIS VULGAR DISPLAY OF ILLUSTRATION POWER HAS ENDED

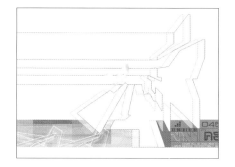

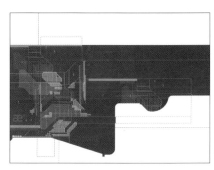

Ae 045
Creative Blood

Fig.1

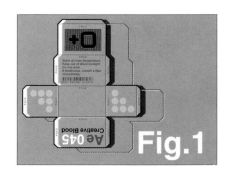

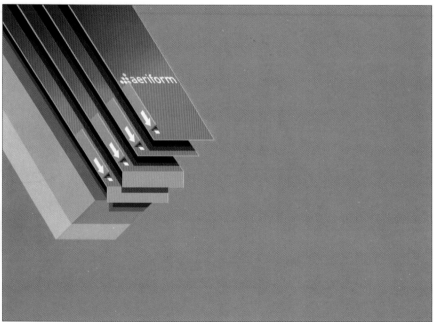

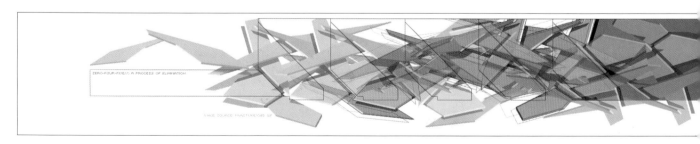

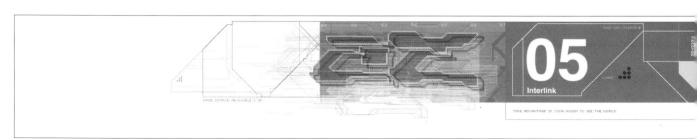

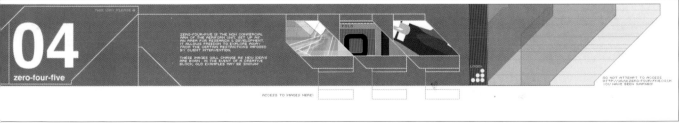

04

zero-four-five

ZERO-FOUR-FIVE IS THE NON COMMERCIAL
ARM OF THE AERIFORM UNIT, SET UP AS
AN AREA FOR RESEARCH & DEVELOPMENT.
IT ALLOWS FREEDOM TO EXPLORE AWAY
FROM THE CERTAIN RESTRICTIONS IMPOSED
BY CLIENT INTERVENTION.

THESE IMAGES WILL CHANGE AS NEW IDEA'S
ARE BORN. IN THE EVENT OF A CREATIVE
BLOCK, OLD EXAMPLES MAY BE SHOWN.

ACCESS TO IMAGES HERE!

DO NOT ATTEMPT TO ACCESS
HTTP://WWW.ZERO-FOUR-FIVE.CO.UK
(YOU HAVE BEEN WARNED!)

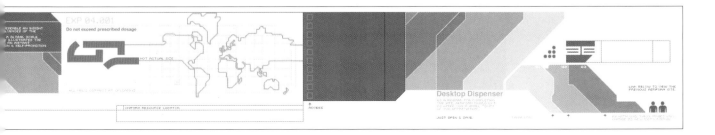

EXP 04.001

Do not exceed prescribed dosage

NOT ACTUAL SIZE

Desktop Dispenser

UNIFORM RESOURCE LOCATOR

JUST OPEN & DRINK

LINK BELOW TO VIEW THE
PREVIOUS AERIFORM SITE.

ONE9INE

New York
www.one9ine.com

The design studio One9ine was started by Matt Owens and Warren Corbitt; they specialize in visual communications for print, broadcast, and interactive media. With a broad base of skills and knowledge, which includes editorial design, brand-identity development, website development, consulting, and creative direction, the One9ine studio works in several different media. Their portfolio website displays several of their projects for a list of clients, including various museums and public institutions. The central graphic of the website's main interface page is a "three-dimensional" cross. The navigation bar is a horizontal, floating menu that appears and disappears as the mouse is dragged over the field. One9ine's individual projects are organized by pop-up windows that float above the central cross—the user's fixed virtual position. The site's information passes between the two in a stream. This setup is not unique to the One9ine site, but is a good example of the newly simplified possibilities for website organization.

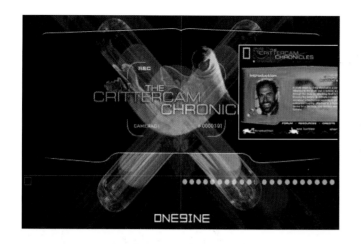

THE CRITTERCAM CHRONIC

ONE9INE

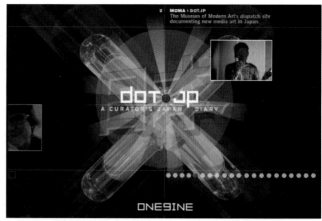

MOMA > DOT.JP
The Museum of Modern Art's dispatch site documenting new media art in Japan.

dot.jp
A CURATOR'S JAPAN DIARY

ONE9INE

DEEPEND : EMIGRE SPREADS
Five spreads for Emigre magazine on the topic of the creative endeavour.

ONE9INE

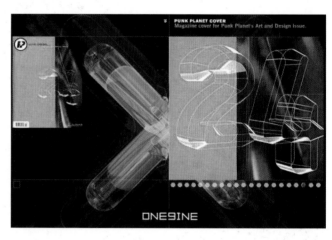

PUNK PLANET COVER
Magazine cover for Punk Planet's Art and Design issue.

ONE9INE

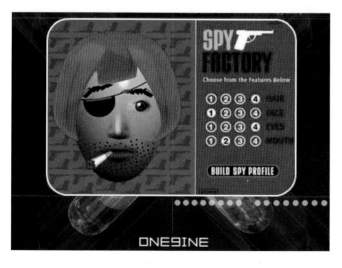

Redesign of Raygun Magazine, cover and select spreads. co-designed with Barry Deck.

style
smile

ONE9INE

one9ine is a studio committed to excellence in design across media. As print, interactive, and broadcast media converge, design remains the fundamental conduit between client and audience. At one9ine, creativity, and technology respond to one another, both to build value and to form new avenues for visual communication.

Above all, creative work should have an energy and freshness of approach that makes the client, audience, and designer excited and engaged. one9ine focuses on developing smart, successful ideas and on maintaining the highest level of inspiration and sophistication from project to project.

MORE >>

ONE9INE

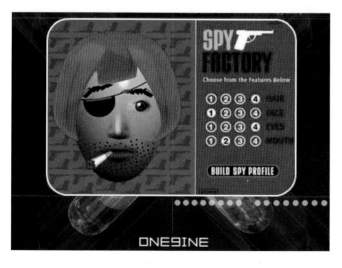

SPY FACTORY
Choose from the Features Below
① ② ③ ④ HAIR
① ② ③ ④ FACE
① ② ③ ④ EYES
① ② ③ ④ MOUTH
BUILD SPY PROFILE

ONE9INE

SPY FACTORY
Choose from the Features Below
① ② ③ ④ HAIR
① ② ③ ④ FACE
① ② ③ ④ EYES
① ② ③ ④ MOUTH
BUILD SPY PROFILE

ONE9INE

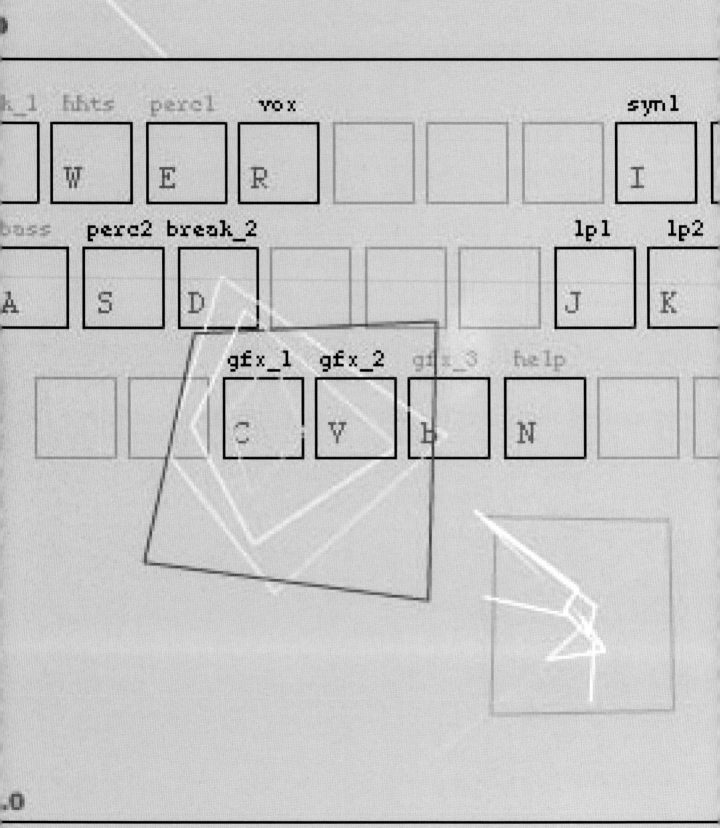

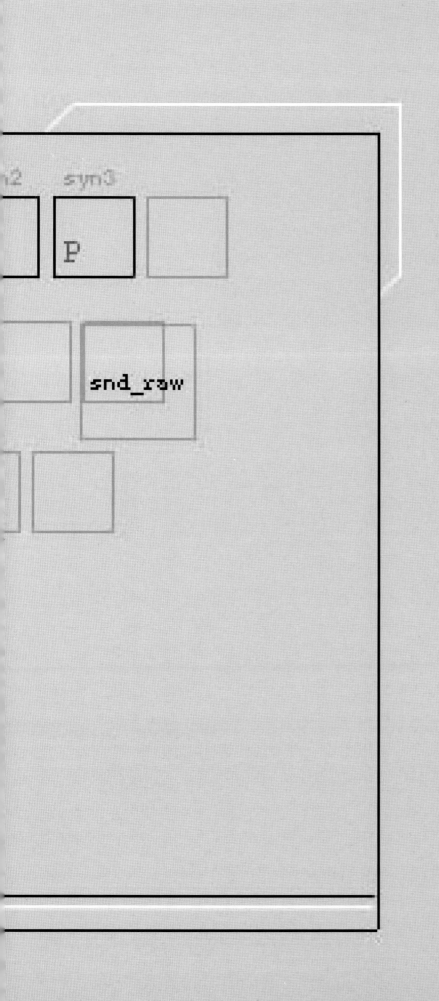

PRAYSTATION

Port Washington, New York
www.praystation.com

The Praystation site has been in a state of evolution since its initial broadcast in 1998. The site was originally intended to be an affront to religion, offering a place for on-line confession. But the site's first incarnation took the form of a virtual, rotating, "three-dimensional" voodoo doll—an alternative to e-greetings. In the following year, the site featured collages made from video-game imagery and characters, before assuming its current shape: an on-line calendar with highlighted dates, noting events and (more commonly) postings of new material by the site's creator, Joshua Davis. Though the range of topics is broad, the material of each posting is focused and always rather cerebral: studies of software behavior, for example, or a consideration of web design in terms of fractals. The postings, which are open-source, contribute to the larger discourse of the web's function, revealing the creator's respect for the internet as a tool of communication and as a medium for change. In all, the site is a documentation of a process of evolution, an open-ended equation with an unspecified number of variables. Davis is always aware of the site's uncharted movement forward. The use of the calendar underscores the presentation of his efforts not as accomplishments of goals achieved, but rather as steps on a limitless path.

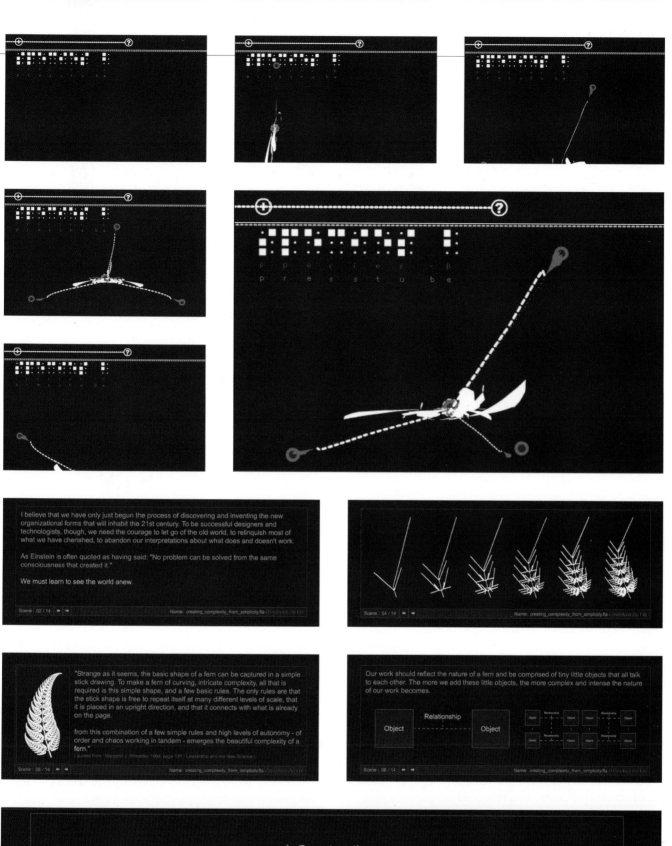
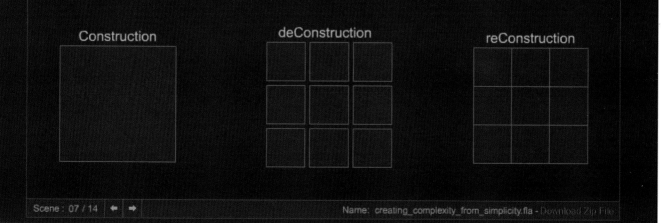

"Mentalities and Anomalies"
1. mode or way of thought 2. deviation from the common rule / something different, abnormal, peculiar, or not easily classified.

by Joshua Davis

http://www.cyphen.com | http://www.praystation.com | http://www.once-upon-a-forest.com

Unite : Commemorate : Explore | http://www.dreamless.org | http://www.antiweb-chaos.com

Kioken Incorporated : Senior Design Technologist | http://www.kioken.com

Scene : 01 / 13

The Mysteries of Harris Burdick by Chris Van Allsburg

When Chris Van Allsburg was invited to the home of Peter Wenders, he discovered fourteen drawings that were, like pieces of a picture puzzle, clues to larger pictures. But the puzzles, the mysteries, presented by these drawings, are not what we are used to, they are not solved for us, as in the final pages of a book or a film's last reel. The solutions to these mysteries lie in a place at once closer at hand, yet far more remote.

They lie in our imagination.

Scene : 02 / 13

The House on Maple Street
It was a perfect lift-off.

Scene : 05 / 13

The Seven Chairs
The fifth one ended up in France.

Scene : 06 / 13

Passion and determination do not slide by unnoticed.

2. You probably won't believe it, but I'm terrible at math. In the late 80's I was a sponsored amateur skateboarder, trust me - I wasn't going to math class. If only my instructors had used flash to demonstrate principals in math, I would have felt infinitely more excited about going to class.

So what I do is something I call "Slam Mathematics". Slam Mathematics is not understanding math.

So I make an object, times by two, then divide it by a million, then do this, then do that, and what happens is - you get accidents, and in those accidents you find things.

Which leads me to my next idea :

Scene : 08 / 13

3. I have no idea what I'm doing.

Now this is the most important out of all of these, because in my not understanding, I find these accidents. My mother gave me this quote once : "It is more rewarding to explore than to reach conclusions, more satisfying to wonder than to know, and more exciting to search than to stay put."

I've tried to carry this idea with me through my life. When I was a kid, living at home with my parents, one day I walked into my mothers kitchen, when no one was home.

I opened this cupboard, and found this box of food coloring. I read the box, finding the words "non-toxic" written on the side. So I took out one of the bottles, unscrewed the cap, and dropped a few drops into each one of my eyes.

Scene : 09 / 13

Now, for about 20 seconds, I choose red, the entire world is tinted red. I don't suggest that you try this, but if you do, e-mail me - it's wicked.

On this same principal. When I was in college, I was studying to be an illustrator. I was doing these oil paintings on paper and I wanted to know what would happen if I set them on fire. So I started setting all of my artwork on fire. What I found out was, that when I mixed these two oil based resins, and heat was applied, they would separate from each other and create cracks.

I could then bake my artwork in the oven, preheated at 450, the resins would crack, and then I would rub the entire painting with black oil paint. After the entire painting was black, I would take a dry cloth and gently wipe the painting clean. This would take the paint off of the top layer, but leaving the paint within all of the cracks. So I could create these modern paintings, yet make them look hundreds of years old.

Scene : 10 / 13

The lesson is, that I didn't know how to get there. That I needed to set my paintings on fire in order to observe an effect. So not understanding is ok, it tells us that we are still open to explore ideas, that in our mistakes and failures we may discover new things.

So with all of this said, What's your mentality ? What's your philosophy ? What are you thinking about ?

What an exciting medium we work in. I didn't buy a television until fairly recently, and I bought it really only to play video games. So the other day I turn on the TV and this news show is on, and this man says : "Should Bob die ? Log onto our web-site and vote." Sheesh, I stood frozen and continued to watch. Sure enough, after thirty minutes, the man comes back on and says : "80 percent of you said Bob should die "

At that moment I realized how we are totally based in anonymity, and dammit people wanted to be heard.

Scene : 11 / 13

29

years old...and still screaming

06.13.2000

The Harp

So it's true he thought, it's really true.

Scene : 03 / 13 ◄ ►

Archie Smith, Boy Wonder

A tiny voice asked, "Is he the one?".

Scene : 04 / 13 ◄ ►

Lets begin by touching base on a few misconceptions.

1. Several people have come up to me, and have also received through e-mail, that they think PrayStation is a team of people - and it's just me, one guy. I think that this is important because - Matt Owens, of volumeone.com, my friend and neighbor told me once; **"That we have grown up on the Fugazi - do it yourself mentality"**. So what I think this says to us is that for commercial work, teams may need to be assembled, but for own personal work and exploration - anyone can do what I'm doing.

Joe from joecartoon.com said at FlashForward2000 in New York City, that he worked in a corporate environment, and when the day was over, his co-workers would stop what they were doing and would go home, plop in front of the television, go to sleep, and then get up for work the next day. However, Joe would get off work, go home, and spend several more hours doing the same exact stuff but for himself.

Scene : 07 / 13 ◄ ►

The experience doesn't seem all there yet.

Having to leave one experience to interact with another experience, to view your results back on the previous experience.

At one point in history - the theater was 100% of societies evening entertainment. This experience fell by the wayside, movie theaters and home entertainment (surround sound systems and dvd) replaced the experience of the past. There is no doubt that our medium is the next experience. I choose to use Flash because of its possibilities in movement, sound and interaction.

Time will tell and who knows to what extent this will evolve.

Scene : 12 / 13 ◄ ►

So this got me thinking about the idea of foundation, what did I need to lay down in order to build upon a body of work? Up until quite recently, I thought foundation was something that existed in the past. Now I believe that the past is only for education of what to do and not to do on future endeavors.

Foundation actually exists in the moment, **something we are constantly updating.**

If you build a building, maintenance must be constantly applied to your foundation, in order for the small individual experiences to remain in motion. The minute maintenance on the foundation stops, your building crumbles from the wear of time and external forces.

So, while some people might be concerned with keeping things within the realm of usability blandness - **"that which does not change, dies"**. This experience isn't figured out and change, accidents, being confused, and exploration is what's making this work an exciting medium to be in.

Scene : 13 / 13 ◄ ►

Dreamless.org

is alive and kicking.

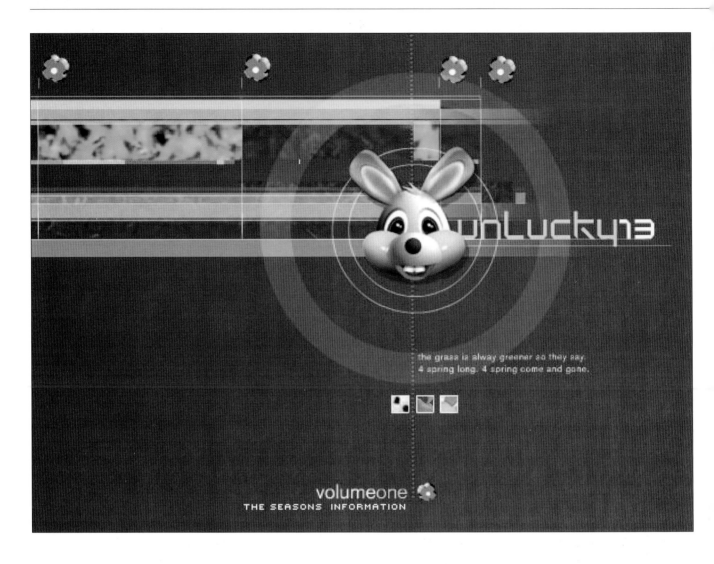

New York
www.volumeone.com

The gamut of images and topics at the Volume One site ensures that each release of the quarterly magazine will be a surprise for the user. The story itself develops from the ad-hoc selection of visual elements: a jihad with power-tools, a swimmer, or a grinning stuffed animal. The unconventional narrative structure uses looping sequences, which are complex structures of moving images, sounds, and texts. Volume One is an independent site; its creator, Matt Owens, uses it for exploring narrative and design in tandem with his work on commercial projects. On the development of a story line in the context of a website, Owens writes, "With the advent of Flash, I have been able to really explore the cinematic and narrative qualities of interactive design and storytelling. With Volume One, I wanted to create a place to design and explore ideas outside of client constraints. I update it four times a year; this way I always have a deadline. . . .The end result is an ever-growing range of projects. I try to do different things and develop a merge of visual and technological ideas."

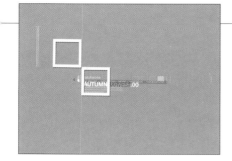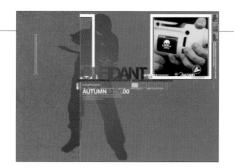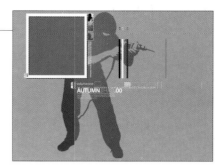

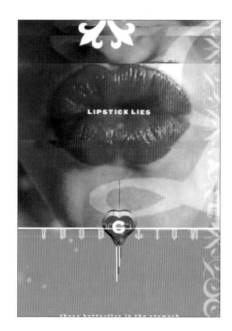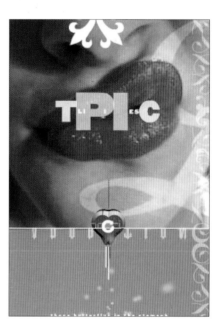

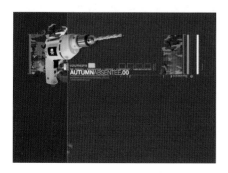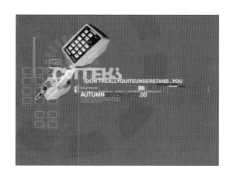

SOULBATH

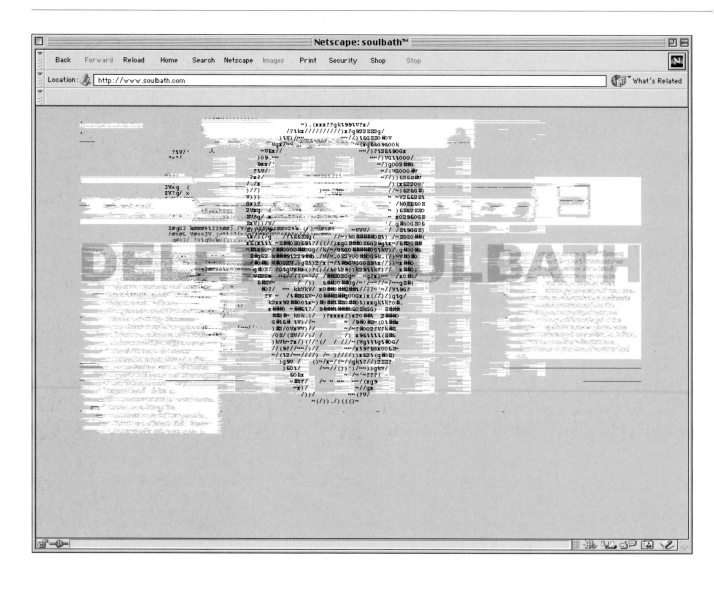

London
www.soulbath.com

Web-designers Florian Schmitt and Alexandra Jugovic have created Soulbath as an auxiliary site to their Hi-Res! website. Soulbath is something like an organized junkyard for web design. In the site's navigations through the technically complex functions, there are detours to error messages and dead ends, an intentional sabotage of the "safe and controlled experience" provided by most websites, as Schmitt explains. The navigation never allows the user to have a sense of full control, and the built-in pitfalls are meant to be unsettling. Similarly, the text on the site is perplexing: an unedited stream of writings—mostly having to do with theory of some unspecified nature—roughly put together from secondary sources. To further complicate this "digital frame" of texts, the function "Clickhere!" allows users to post their own selection of writings, to continue a successive chain of users' contributed texts. But just as it is engaged with teasing the user, the Soulbath site also functions as a laboratory for new design, which makes for a bizarre combination of polished programming and raw material. For the site, Schmitt and Jugovic also created a gallery of actual and fake banners—exhibited in a virtual five-story complex—the perspective of which changes as the user moves between floors. The look of sophisticated display graphics in such a context is somewhat jarring, like the appearance of an overdressed guest at an informal party. It is all, however, part of the designers' master plan. For Soulbath's creators, well-charted and well-contained web environments are as uninteresting as an artificial garden.

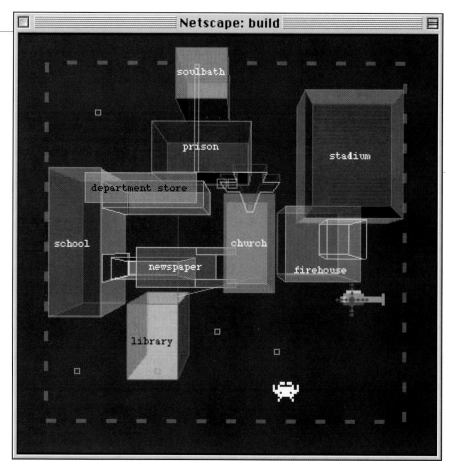

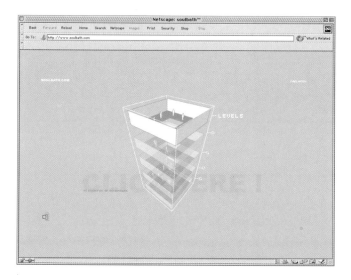

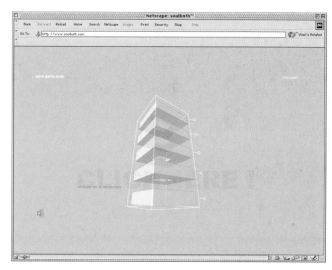

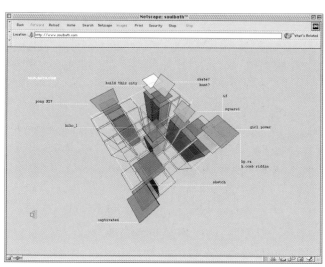

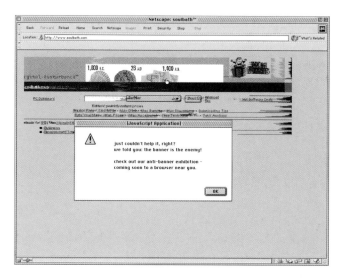

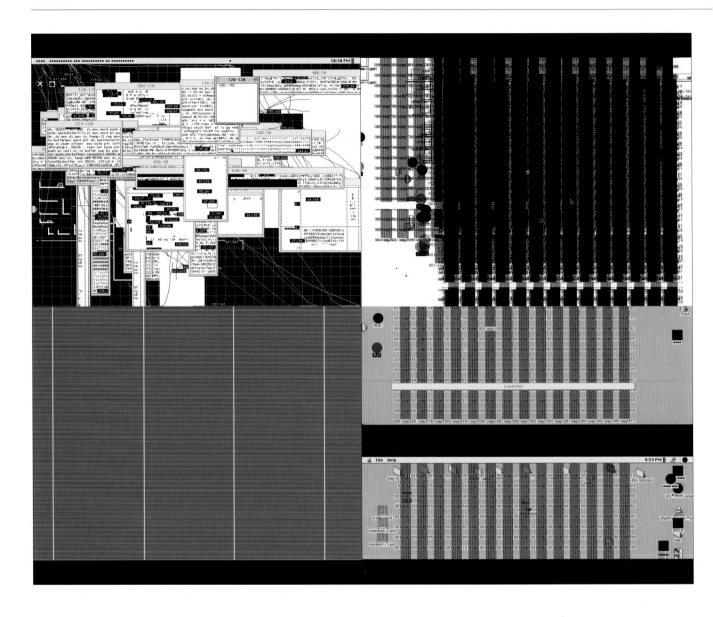

Barcelona
www.jodi.org

Jodi is the creation of Dirk Paesmans and Joan Heemskerk. The site challenges the formal trappings of what are now widely accepted as the standards of website construction, and the role of the internet as mass media. And in the site's massive content, there is just enough disorientation for the user to forget the port of entry. Once in, there is a succession of links that hurdle the user through limitless and totally different pages. Frustration is unavoidable as the mind trips through a veritable guessing game of what to do, how to behave, and what the site could possibly mean; every encounter with a rollover or hypertext must be considered and (often) summarily dismissed. But this provocation is a signal that our preconceptions of websites and web function are being shaken up—thankfully. Not surprisingly, the site has been maligned by users and providers as having "no content," and as being unintelligible because of its lack of user-friendly navigation or "safe" content. (This resistance has meant that Jodi must continually change providers.) Launched in 1994 as part of a new wave of "weird" websites, Jodi nonetheless continues to grow in size and has become well-respected by web artists and designers alike. The flickering screens, scramble of texts in various sizes, and blocks of color make up the visual content and provide a welcome escape from the systems of knowledge, coding of information, and rapid visual assimilation that have become so prevalent in website design.

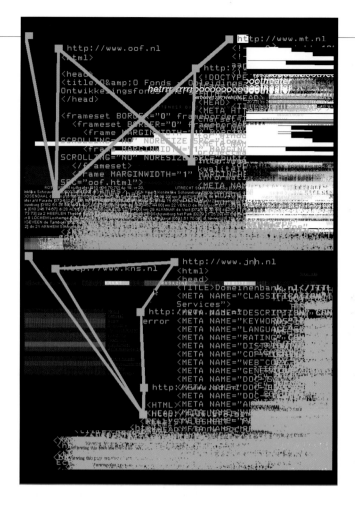

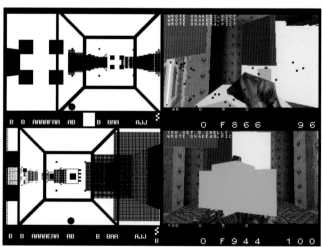

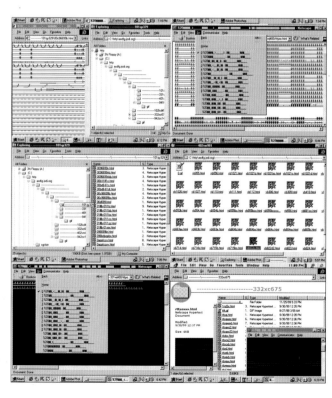

contact

www. rhizome.org

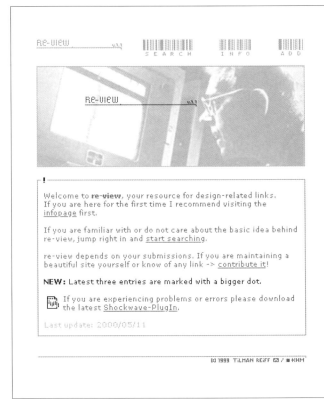

www.re-source.com/re-view

www.webtype.org

www.digitalthread.com

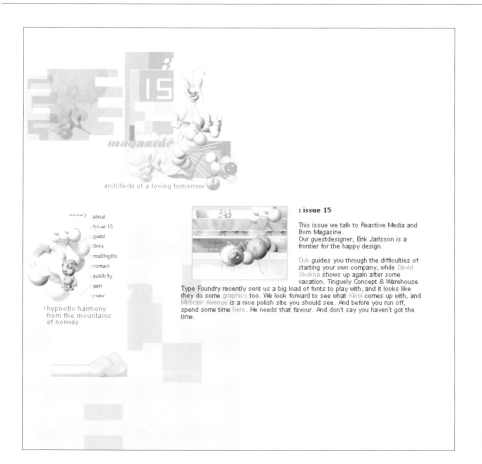

: issue 15

This issue we talk to Reactive Media and Born Magazine.
Our guestdesigner, Erik Jarlsson is a frontier for the happy design.

Dub guides you through the difficulties of starting your own company, while David Skokna shows up again after some vacation. Tinguely Concept & Warehouse Type Foundry recently sent us a big load of fonts to play with, and it looks like they do some graphics too. We look forward to see what Kiiroi comes up with, and Mebrain Avenue is a nice polish site you should see. And before you run off, spend some time here. He needs that favour. And don't say you haven't got the time.

www.tricom.no/sabre/s.htm

www.threeoh.com

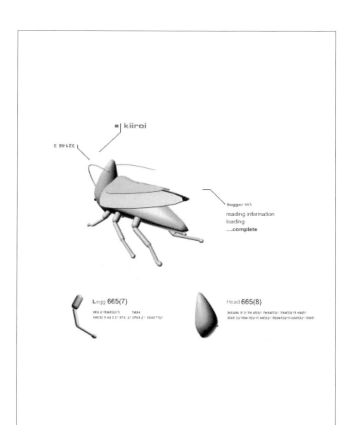

www.kiiroi.nu

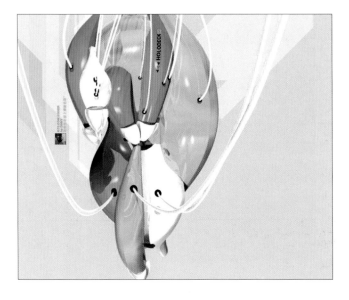

www.h73.com

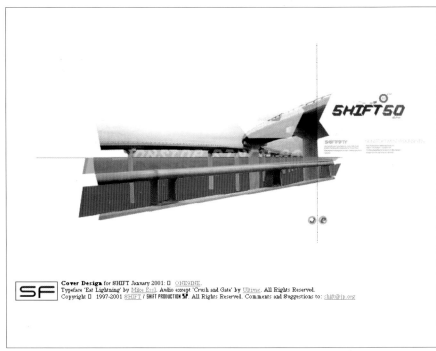

www.shift.jp.org (Cover by One9ine)

www.vtwinlabs.com

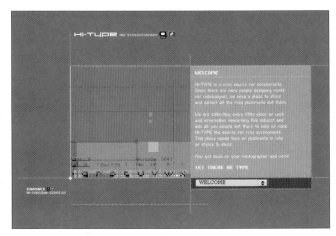

www.hi-type.de

www.sinnzeug.de

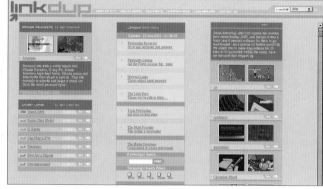

www.linkdup.com

www.creativebase.com

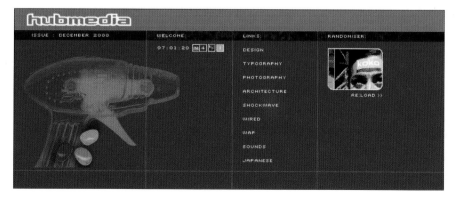

www.hubmedia.co.uk

INDEX & DIRECTORY

The preparation of **Now Loading . . .** has involved a lot of collaboration, without which completion of this volume would not have been possible. I would like to thank the designers and creators of the sites for their generosity of spirit, time, and consideration. Also, as a token of my gratitude, I would like to list the individuals who have provided invaluable advice, commentary, as well as reams of links: Emiko Yoshise, Emiko Akamatsu, Katsuya Moriizumi, Rico Komanoya and Masanori Omae of DEX, Andrew Wilcox of Spike, Kyoko Wada, Shuzo Hayashi of Lim Lam Design, and Lesley Ann Martin. I would like to express special thanks to Julian Stevens for his continued support and enthusiasm, lucid insights on the web, web design, and for his fantastic links.

A note on the use of works:

All the illustrations that appear in this volume have been used with knowledge and permission of the designer or creator for usage explicitly limited to reproduction in this volume. All other reproduction and subsidiary rights are reserved by the designers and creators. For further information or requests please contact the websites directly. All the images that appear in this book are screengrabs. Apart from cropping, there has been no alteration or manipulation of any of the images.

The typeface used throughout this volume is called **Techno**.

COPYRIGHT NOTICE

Published in the United States in 2001 by

Gingko Press Inc.

5768 Paradise Drive, Suite J

Corte Madera, CA 94925

Phone: (415) 924-9615 Fax: (415) 924-9608 USA

e-mail: books@gingkopress.com

http://www.gingkopress.com

ISBN 1-58423-077-0

Published in Japan, Korea, Taiwan, and mainland China in 2001 by

DesignEXchange Company Limited

BR Takanawa 3-12-8 Takanawa

Minato-ku Tokyo 108-0074 Japan

Phone: 81 3 5798 0216 Fax: 81 3 5798 0212

e-mail:intl@dex.ne.jp

http://www.dex.ne.jp

Author, editor, research, book design and layout: **Ivan Vartanian**

Production, Co-edition control, and Marketing: **Rico Komanoya**

Copyediting: **Diana C. Stoll**

Additional proofreading: **Donna Wiemann**

Project initiation: **Gingko Press**

Printed in Hong Kong by Everbest Printing Company Limited

First Printing, 2001